London's AFTERNOON TEAS

A Guide to the Most Exquisite Tea Venues in London

REVISED & EXPANDED 2ND EDITION

SUSAN COHEN

IMM **lifestyle** books™

Read. Learn. Do What You Love.

Published 2018—IMM Lifestyle Books
www.IMMLifestyleBooks.com

IMM Lifestyle Books are distributed in the UK by Grantham Book Service,
Trent Road, Grantham, Lincolnshire, NG31 7XQ.

In North America, IMM Lifestyle Books are distributed by Fox Chapel Publishing,
903 Square Street, Mount Joy, PA 17552, *www.FoxChapelPublishing.com*.

London's Afternoon Teas, Revised & Expanded 2nd Edition (2018) is a completely
revised edition of *London's Afternoon Teas* (2014), published by IMM Lifestyle
Books. Revisions include all new photographs, all new venues, and all new text.

ISBN 978-1-5048-0088-4

Library of Congress Cataloging-in-Publication Data

Names: Cohen, Susan, 1946–
Title: London's afternoon teas / Susan Cohen.
Description: Revised & expanded 2nd edition. | Mount Joy [Pennsylvania] : IMM
    Lifestyle Books, 2018. | Includes index.
Identifiers: LCCN 2017054677 | ISBN 9781504800884
Subjects: LCSH: Tearooms—England—London—Guidebooks.
Classification: LCC TX907.5.B7 C646 2018 | DDC 642—dc23
LC record available at https://lccn.loc.gov/2017054677

We are always looking for talented authors. To submit an idea, please send a brief
inquiry to acquisitions@foxchapelpublishing.com.

Printed in China
10 9 8 7 6 5 4 3 2 1

Introduction

There is nowhere better in the world to enjoy the quintessentially English custom of afternoon tea than London, the most vibrant and exciting capital city in the world. London has the most amazing selection of venues where you can indulge yourself and partake of anything from the most time-honoured afternoon teas to the newest twists on tradition.

Tea can be a late lunch or an early supper, in which case high tea fits the bill perfectly, with savoury items to add a bit more substance. You may be looking for a conventional afternoon tea of scones with lashings of clotted cream and fruity jam, luscious cakes, and finger sandwiches—without crusts, and there has to be cucumber. Perhaps you fancy a more savoury repast, or are searching for a tea designed with the carnivore in mind, or where there is whisky, gin, beer, or sake as well as tea to drink. Not forgetting that tea is often a family outing, there are plenty of venues which will appeal to parents and children alike. Maybe you are after a variation on a theme, whether it be an afternoon tea bus tour of London, an Alice in Wonderland–inspired afternoon tea, or a tea where your pooch can enjoy his or her own delicious doggy tea.

Whatever your taste, London can provide it all, and in an array of interesting and exciting locations. After all, the afternoon tea experience is not just about the food you

eat and the tea you drink, but also about the space and place; in this city, fashion and style have had a powerful influence on afternoon tea. You can enjoy your afternoon tea in buildings steeped in history, from Georgian townhouses, resplendent in modern décor, to chic and buzzy bars. From elegant drawing rooms and opulent lounges in the grandest of hotels to French-style brasseries and the top of an iconic red London bus, there is somewhere to suit everyone, every budget, and every occasion. There are venues with spectacular views, others with light and bright conservatories, and even one, favoured by royalty, with a terrace overlooking a glorious private garden.

Whether you want to linger and chat with friends, have a business meeting in relaxed surroundings, commemorate a birthday or anniversary, collapse after a day's shopping, or indulge in a pre-theatre high tea, the capital can provide the ideal location. Do not despair if you are venturing out of London, for you'll find some selected places not far from the capital where you can enjoy an equally good afternoon tea. Afternoon tea is the perfect way to mark those special dates in the calendar, from Valentine's Day to Mother's Day, Easter to Halloween, and through to Christmas. Then there are the great British annual social events, like Wimbledon week, the Chelsea Flower Show, and the Henley Royal Regatta; many of the venues in this book offer themed teas which celebrate these particular events. This guidebook is here to help you make your choice.

How afternoon tea started

*T*avistock, Devon, staked its claim as the birthplace of the cream tea back in the early 11th century. The Benedictine Abbey had been looted by the Vikings in 997 AD, and a century later the monks rewarded the labourers who worked to restore it with a meal of bread, clotted cream, and strawberry preserve. The Devon cream tea proved so popular that the monks continued to serve it to passing travellers long after the builders had left.

It is uncertain whether Anna Maria, the seventh Duchess of Bedford, partook of scones and cream, but according to legend, it was she who was responsible for the invention of afternoon tea as an 'event' in the 1840s. The story goes that she was so hungry in the long gap between lunch and dinner at 9 o'clock in the evening that she ordered her maid to serve tea and cakes at 5 o'clock to alleviate her gnawing hunger pains. It was not long before afternoon tea became de riguer in London society.

As for the drink itself, high society also played their part in making tea central to the ritual. Tea was given the royal seal of approval by Catherine of Braganza, the Portuguese wife of King Charles II, who brought a chest of tea with her as part of her dowry in 1662. Queen Victoria's Prime Minister, William Gladstone, captured the very essence of tea when he wrote these words in 1865: 'Relaxing, refreshing, stimulating, or warming, there is little to compare with the comfort and delights of a steaming pot of tea'.

There is a certain magical, even mystical quality about tea, not least of all because of the amazing influence the tiny leaf exerts on everyday life. A cup of tea is the best reason in the world to stop for a break during the day. Life's rites of passage would not be the

same without tea, and the variety of leaves is such that every mood and taste can be catered for. As the world's most popular drink, tea crosses all the boundaries of history, nation, culture, and class. At some time in their lives, most people, even the smallest children, acquire a 'taste' for tea, a habit that they rarely relinquish. The combination of a beautifully presented afternoon feast and freshly brewed leaf tea served in porcelain or bone china cups is a marriage made in heaven and an experience to be savoured.

The 21st century has seen afternoon tea gain an unprecedented popularity, with London serving as the mecca for the revival. Across the capital, venues in abundance create wonderful, often innovative menus, serve exquisite food and drink in perfect surroundings, and rely on the expertise of professionals to ensure you enjoy the best experience possible. Many of the venues have won prestigious awards, confirming their dedication to high standards.

No longer the preserve of ladies on a shopping trip or families celebrating a special occasion, afternoon tea has become a favourite pastime enjoyed by anyone and everyone, an up-to-the-minute sociable thing to do. The synergy of design, fashion, and food has had a wonderful impact and resulted in an exciting new genre, with afternoon teas on offer suited to every generation and to people from all walks of life. If you are a visitor to the capital, what better time-honoured British tradition could you choose to experience, and for the local, what better excuse could there be to leave the hustle and bustle of everyday life behind for a few hours? Afternoon tea is about treating yourself, your friends, and your family, either informally or in luxurious style, so find a venue that strikes your fancy and enjoy yourself.

Contents

11 Cadogan Gardens. 12

The Ampersand 14

• RECIPE: White Chocolate Scones. . . . 16

The Athenaeum Hotel. 18

Balthazar 22

The Berkeley 25

Biscuiteers 28

The Bloomsbury 31

Brigit's Bakery. 33

Brigit's Bakery Afternoon Tea
    Bus and Boat Tours. 35

Brown's Hotel 38

Claridge's. 41

Cliveden House (Taplow, Berkshire). . 44

The Connaught 48

Conrad London St James 52

Corinthia Hotel. 55

Coworth Park (Ascot, Berkshire) 58

Dean Street Townhouse 62

The Dorchester 65

Egerton House Hotel 68

• RECIPE: Cape Seed Loaf 70

Fortnum & Mason 72

Four Seasons Hotel, Park Lane 76

• RECIPE: Lemon Cake with
    Rhubarb and Vanilla Filling. 78

Four Seasons Hotel, Ten Trinity
    Square 80

The Goring 83

• RECIPE: Mince Pies 86

Grosvenor House. 88

Ham Yard Hotel 92

Hotel Café Royal. 94

Hotel du Vin, Cambridge
    (Cambridge, Cambridgeshire). 97

Hotel du Vin, Henley-on-Thames
    (Henley-on-Thames, Berkshire) . . . 100

InterContinental London, The O2 . . 104

InterContinental London,
  Park Lane 107
• RECIPE: Buttermilk Scones 110
The Ivy, Chelsea Garden 112
The Ivy Café, St John's Wood 115
Kensington Palace 117
The Lanesborough 119
• RECIPE: Rocher Praline 122
The Langham 124
• RECIPE: Paris Brest 128
Mandarin Oriental 130
Marriott Hotel, County Hall 132
The Milestone Hotel 135
• RECIPE: Shortbread 138
Mondrian London 140
The Ned 142
Number Sixteen 145
Old Parsonage Hotel (Oxford,
  Oxfordshire) 147
• RECIPE: Macarons 150
One Aldwych 152

OXO Tower Restaurant 155
The Petersham (Richmond, Surrey) . . 158
The Ritz 160
Rosewood London 164
The Rubens at the Palace 166
• RECIPE: Brazil Nut Cake 170
Sanctum Soho Hotel 172
Sanderson 175
The Savoy 178
sketch 182
Sofitel London St James 186
The Soho Hotel 190
St Martins Lane 192
St Pancras Renaissance Hotel 195
The Stafford 197
The Wallace Restaurant 200
The Wellesley, Knightsbridge 203
The Wolseley 205

Credits 207
Index 207

Map of tea venues

1 11 Cadogan Gardens
2 The Ampersand
3 The Athenaeum Hotel
4 Balthazar
5 The Berkeley
6 Biscuiteers
7 The Bloomsbury
8 Brigit's Bakery
9 Brigit's Bakery Afternoon
   Tea Bus and Boat Tours
10 Brown's Hotel
11 Claridge's
12 The Connaught
13 Conrad London St James
14 Corinthia Hotel
15 Dean Street Townhouse
16 The Dorchester
17 Egerton House Hotel
18 Fortnum & Mason
19 Four Seasons Hotel, Park Lane

20 Four Seasons Hotel,
   Ten Trinity Square
21 The Goring
22 Grosvenor House
23 Ham Yard Hotel
24 Hotel Café Royal
25 InterContinental London, The O2
26 InterContinental London, Park Lane
27 The Ivy, Chelsea Garden
28 The Ivy Café, St John's Wood
29 Kensington Palace
30 The Lanesborough
31 The Langham
32 Mandarin Oriental
33 Marriott Hotel, County Hall
34 The Milestone Hotel
35 Mondrian London
36 The Ned
37 Number Sixteen
38 One Aldwych

39 OXO Tower Restaurant
40 The Ritz
41 Rosewood London
42 The Rubens at the Palace
43 Sanctum Soho Hotel
44 Sanderson
45 The Savoy
46 sketch
47 Sofitel London St James
48 The Soho Hotel
49 St Martins Lane
50 St Pancras Renaissance Hotel
51 The Stafford
52 The Wallace Restaurant
53 The Wellesley, Knightsbridge
54 The Wolseley

Venues Outside of London

Cliveden (Taplow, Berkshire)

Coworth Park (Ascot, Berkshire)

Hotel du Vin
(Cambridge, Cambridgeshire)

Hotel du Vin
(Henley-on-Thames, Berkshire)

Old Parsonage Hotel
(Oxford, Oxfordshire)

The Petersham (Richmond, Surrey)

11 CADOGAN GARDENS

*J*ust a short walk from Sloane Square, stroll along a leafy street of grand terraced houses, and once you've conquered the curious numbering system, you'll find 11 Cadogan Gardens. Behind the Victorian façade is one of London's best-kept secrets, a gem of a destination for afternoon tea. Quintessentially English, the interior is dramatic, eclectic, and quirky, and whilst the furnishings are traditional, they have a distinctively modern twist to them. Guests generally take their afternoon tea in the flower-filled Drawing Room, but a small party of four to five people can also be seated in the conservatory. The terrace is a lovely option on a sunny day, and if you are a bigger party of eight to ten, then you can make an advance booking for the Library. The Drawing Room has a comfortable, cosy feel to it, and retains all the original features, including the large stone fireplace. But there is nothing Victorian about the furniture, which features stylish, contemporary, polished wood tables and

ADDRESS: 11 Cadogan Gardens, Chelsea, London SW3 2RJ

TEL: +44 (0)20 7730 7000

EMAIL: reservations@11cadogangardens.com

WEB: www.11cadogangardens.com

AFTERNOON TEA SERVED: daily 2.30pm–6.00pm

SET TEAS: champagne afternoon tea, seasonal special teas. Dietary requirements including vegetarian, vegan, and gluten free can be catered for; advance notice is preferred. Advance booking is highly recommended.

NEAREST UNDERGROUND STATIONS: Sloane Square

PLACES OF INTEREST NEARBY: Sloane Street shopping, Saatchi Gallery, Royal Hospital Chelsea, Ranelagh Gardens, Chelsea Physic Garden

elegant upholstered chairs. Begin with a complimentary glass of Taittinger Champagne, and choose your leaf tea from the menu or the additional list. Tuck into the deliciously light sandwiches, followed by scones with jam and clotted cream. To complete the treat, there is a selection of beautifully crafted dainty pastries, accompanied by a shot glass filled with a fruit soup, maybe mango, topped with a yogurt foam. The hotel puts on a lovely festive tea at Christmas, which is served from late November to late December, and in May, it's worth looking out for their Chelsea Flower Show flower-inspired tea. It's altogether a super place to have a really good, well-priced afternoon tea.

THE AMPERSAND

*J*ust minutes away from three of London's most famous museums, the light and airy Drawing Rooms within Kensington's Ampersand Hotel are the perfect place for an excellent afternoon tea inspired by the Science Museum. The stylish décor is a combination of English drawing room and salon de thé, with richly upholstered deep sofas and comfortable armchairs, and helpful, friendly staff will guide you through the menu and the teas on offer.

Rather than the usual sandwiches, the chef has come up with a super selection of delicious variations on the savoury course. Expect filled miniature gougère or generously topped bite-sized tartines, seasonal mini quiches, or tiny bagels or blinis topped with smoked salmon and avocado. Follow these with warm scones, both plain and studded with white chocolate, served with clotted cream and homemade strawberry jam, before you get to the pastries, which are the star turn and bound to entrance any children in your party. The Natural History Museum gets a nod here with the shortbread dinosaur biscuits, but science is the overriding theme, with

changes to the menu made from time to time. There might be a Milky Way macaron or a chocolate mint planet, and you get to experiment with test tubes full of colored crystals, chocolate pearls, and toffee sauce, plus cocoa powder to dust over a biscuit and reveal a fossil. Add a glass of champagne for the ultimate treat. This is definitely one of the most entertaining teas in London, and bound to bring a smile to your face, whether you are nine or ninety.

ADDRESS: 10 Harrington Road, South Kensington, London SW7 3ER

TEL: +44 (0)20 7591 4414

EMAIL: drawingrooms@ampersandhotel.com

WEB: www.ampersandhotel.com

AFTERNOON TEA SERVED: Monday to Friday 2.30pm–5.30pm, including bank holidays; weekends 12.30pm–5.30pm

SET TEAS: Science Afternoon Tea, Vegetarian Science Afternoon Tea. A gluten free alternative is available on request on the day.

NEAREST UNDERGROUND STATIONS: South Kensington

PLACES OF INTEREST NEARBY: Royal Albert Hall, Albert Memorial, Kensington Gardens, Hyde Park, Serpentine Gallery, Victoria and Albert Museum, Science Museum, Natural History Museum, Christie's Fine Art and Antiques, Harrods

White Chocolate Scones

Recipe courtesy The Ampersand

INGREDIENTS

- 600 g (4¾ cups + 1 Tbsp.) plain (all-purpose) flour
- 100 g (⅓ cup + 2 Tbsp.) caster (superfine granulated) sugar
- 20 g (1 Tbsp. + 2 tsp.) baking powder
- 2 g (⅓ tsp.) salt
- 150 g (⅔ cup) cold butter, diced
- 2 eggs (100 g/½ cup)
- 220 g (¾ cup + 2 Tbsp.) double cream (heavy cream)
- 200 g (1 cup + 2 Tbsp.) white chocolate baking chips
- Egg wash: lightly beaten egg yolk

*T*his recipe is from head pastry chef Sezwin Mascarenhas.

METHOD

1. Preheat the oven to 180°C (350°F).
2. Lightly grease a baking sheet.
3. In the bowl of a food processor, combine the flour, sugar, baking powder, salt, and butter and, using the paddle attachment, pulse until the mixture resembles fine bread crumbs.
4. Whisk together the eggs and cream and slowly add to the flour mixture to get a soft dough.
5. Turn onto a floured work surface and knead very lightly. Pat out to a circular shape, about 2.5 cm (1 inch) thickness, and rest the dough for 2 hours in the refrigerator.
6. Use a 5 cm (2 inch) cutter to cut out rounds and place on a baking sheet not too close together. Lightly knead together the rest of the dough and cut out more scones to use up all the dough.
7. Brush the tops of the scones with the beaten egg yolk. Bake for 12 to 13 minutes until well risen and golden.
8. Cool on a wire rack and serve with strawberry jam and some clotted cream.

This recipe presents terms and measurements for both UK and US readers. Units are given first for UK readers in the original measurement units, then for US readers in converted units in parentheses. Do not mix the units. US equivalent terms are also given in parentheses where needed.

THE ATHENAEUM HOTEL

*S*ituated in the heart of Mayfair, opposite Green Park, the Athenaeum Hotel is one of London's few family-run five-star hotels, and a complete refurbishment has transformed it into an elegant, modern hotel that retains a home-away-from-home atmosphere. The famed Living Wall on the corner of the building has been extended, and the Michelin-starred Galvin brothers, Chris and Jeff, now head the kitchens. Afternoon tea can be served in the lounge, seated in the more formal Galvin restaurant, or in the comfy bar. Don't be disconcerted by the large TV screen at the far end of this room – it shows major sports events such as Wimbledon and the World and Euro Cups, and when these are not around, you can catch up watching romantic, retro movies, making a connection with the earlier use of the building by the Rank Organisation. There is also an outside terrace on Piccadilly where you can sit and enjoy your tea while you watch the world go by.

The courteous staff take the greatest care of you, from describing the various menus, to helping you choose from the select list of artisan leaf teas, to serving you. Both the sweeter Classic and the Royal teas as well as the more savoury Gentleman's tea showcase the country's very best ingredients, including Cumbrian ham and

ADDRESS: 116 Piccadilly, Mayfair, London W1J 7BJ

TEL: +44 (0)20 7640 3333

EMAIL: galvin@athenaeumhotel.com

WEB: www.athenaeumhotel.com

OFFERS: see www.afternoontea .co.uk/uk/london

AFTERNOON TEA SERVED: Monday to Saturday 12.30 noon–4.30pm, Sunday 12.30 noon–5.30pm. Advance booking advised, especially for the Gentleman's Tea.

SET TEAS: classic, gluten and dairy free, Royal, Gentleman's, occasional seasonal themed afternoon teas

NEAREST UNDERGROUND STATIONS: Green Park, Hyde Park Corner

PLACES OF INTEREST NEARBY: Buckingham Palace, Hyde Park, Green Park, Admiralty Arch, Royal Academy, Burlington Arcade

fresh smoked salmon from Severn & Wye. Sandwiches have delicious and generous fillings on tasty breads, including beetroot, 'pain de mie', and onion, and are replenished as often as you like. The Royal menu features a bridge roll filled with Eggs 'Drumkilbo', a favourite of the late Queen Mother, which is a wonderful concoction of egg and tarragon bound in a lobster mayonnaise, then topped with crayfish and garnished with a sprig of chervil. There is a different selection of delectable pastries on each of the Classic and Royal teas. You can expect the likes of a macaron, delightful fairy cakes, Scottish shortbread, and miniature Eton Mess, with changes reflecting the seasons and produce of the year. Of course there are scones, both fruit and plain, with jolly good house-made preserves and clotted cream. The savoury tea – which of course is not just for gentlemen – has cheese scones with an Alsace bacon butter, a fruit-filled Eccles cake served with a wedge of Lincolnshire poacher cheese and chutney, a Scotch egg whose yolk is cooked to perfection (still slightly runny), a sausage roll

in crisp puff pastry, and a crumpet covered with a delicious Lancashire 'Bomb' cheese rarebit. Should you still have room, there are slices of sourdough toast waiting to have Gentleman's Relish spread on them, all washed down with a dram of the Athenaeum's specially blended Scotch whisky. There is still a slice of proper cake waiting to be eaten, or taken home if you really can't eat it. Everything flows at a leisurely pace and there is never the slightest hint of being rushed, so relax and enjoy the experience.

BALTHAZAR

*T*he famed original Balthazar opened in downtown New York in spring 1997, but London had to wait until early 2013 for the brasserie to finally make its debut in London, right in the heart of Covent Garden and theatreland. This is the only Balthazar outside of Manhattan, and afternoon tea – which you won't find in the New York restaurant – is a very important part of the French-inspired all-day menu. The late 19th-century building has an interesting history, for it was home to the Covent Garden Flower Cellars, where the market traders kept their stock. Then, for many years, the London Theatre Museum was located here, but now the London Film Museum shares the building with Balthazar. The interior décor is ornate, but retains the feel of a typical French brasserie, from the zinc bar, brass rails, and red banquette seating to the bustling atmosphere.

The set afternoon tea menu does change from season to season, and in the past has featured a Bobbi Brown summer tea, inspired by Bobbi's cosmetics, so check out the website to see what is current. Whatever is on the menu will be delicious, for head pastry chef, Régis Beauregard, is a genius at creating divine pastries. Balthazar's High

ADDRESS: 4–6 Russell Street, Covent Garden, London WC2B 5HZ

TEL: +44 (0)20 3301 1155

EMAIL: info@balthazarlondon.com

WEB: www.balthazarlondon.com

AFTERNOON TEA SERVED:
Monday to Friday 3.00pm–5.30pm,
Saturday 3.00pm–5.00pm,
Sunday 3.00pm–6.30pm.
Monday to Sunday during
December 3.00pm–5.00pm

SET TEAS: seasonally changing themed menu, gluten free

NEAREST UNDERGROUND STATIONS: Covent Garden

PLACES OF INTEREST NEARBY: London Film Museum, Covent Garden, Royal Opera House, London Transport Museum, Theatre Royal Drury Lane, Lyceum Theatre, Fortune Theatre, Savoy Theatre, Somerset House

Five afternoon tea, designed to celebrate five years in London, is no exception, featuring the Queen of Tarts, a red, white, and blue macaron which is a salute to the American, British, and French flags, plus the chocolate Balthazar Icon, unmistakably a replica of the famous awning outside. Before you get to these sweet sensations, there are the mouth-watering sandwiches with traditional fillings given a twist, and a really good brioche roll filled with lobster prawn. As tradition demands, there are nicely glazed, light, fruit and plain buttermilk scones, served with rich clotted cream and homemade jam. If you want to dig a bit deeper into your pocket, you could add a real touch of luxury and order 30g (about an ounce) of Imperial caviar, served with blinis and crème fraîche, as well as a glass of champagne or a High Five cocktail. Postcard Teas supply the leaf tea here, and although the list is small, it is very select. Apart from any uneaten treats, which will be boxed up for you if you want, you'll have a lovely take-home gift of an individual cannelé bordelaise. It's up to you how long you hold out before biting into the thin, caramelised shell of this rum-and-vanilla-filled magical confection which is melt-in-the-mouth perfection.

THE BERKELEY

The Collins Room

*T*he Collins Room at The Berkeley is light and bright even on a wet winter's afternoon and is a glorious, elegant place in which to relax and enjoy a very special and unusual afternoon tea. Maybe you have had a hard day shopping or sightseeing; perhaps you want to catch up with some friends; or maybe you simply want to celebrate. Whatever your reason for visiting The Berkeley, the renowned Prêt-à-Portea tea is sure to please. This is a fashionista's delight, and has been firmly fixed on the afternoon tea scene for more than ten years. Each delectable pastry that the hotel's pastry chef produces is a miniature work of art, inspired by the themes and colours of the fashion world. The menu is completely redesigned every six months to follow the changing fashions and styles of the seasons.

The creations, served on delicate, fine bone china designed by Wedgwood, have included Jimmy Choo's monochrome chic Cayla zebra print bag, Moschino's quirky 'Yellow M' handbag of blood orange victoria sponge swathed in red quilted chocolate, and a Valentino sexy sixties mini dress chocolate tartelette filled with caramelia cremeux and whipped ganache, with red and pink chocolate polka dots.

ADDRESS: Wilton Place, Knightsbridge, London SW1X 7RL

TEL: +44 (0)20 7107 8866

EMAIL: dining@the-berkeley.co.uk

WEB: www.the-berkeley.co.uk

AFTERNOON TEA SERVED: daily 1.30pm–5.30pm

SET TEAS: Prêt-à-Portea, Champagne Prêt-à-Portea, Couture Champagne Prêt-à-Portea. Gluten and nut free can be catered for, but please give 24 hours' notice.

DRESS CODE: elegant smart casual; no shorts, vests, sportswear, flip-flops, ripped jeans, or baseball caps

NEAREST UNDERGROUND STATIONS: Knightsbridge, Hyde Park Corner

PLACES OF INTEREST NEARBY: Harvey Nichols, Harrods, Hyde Park, Green Park, Sloane Street and Knightsbridge designer shopping, Natural History Museum, Science Museum, Royal Albert Hall

Guests have also enjoyed a brilliantly British chocolate and vanilla Battenberg cake inspired by Stella McCartney's checkered summer pumps. Breaking with tradition, there are no scones, but your set tea includes a mouth-watering selection of seasonally changing little savouries, tea sandwiches, and stylish canapés. Accompany your Prêt-à-Portea with a glass of champagne or Couture champagne and add a loose-leaf tea chosen from a good selection of savoury and sweet. You'll want to stay all afternoon, but when you finally leave, there is a little Prêt box that is perfect for taking home any unfinished treats. And for those of you who love to bake, you can buy the Prêt-à-Portea book, *High Fashion Bake and Biscuits*, and recreate some of the wonderful pastries at home.

BISCUITEERS

*A*t first glance, you might think this a rather unusual place to visit for afternoon tea, as it is neither a hotel, nor a restaurant, nor a grand café, but it's worth booking in advance to experience Biscuiteers' London Afternoon Tea. Right in the heart of trendy Notting Hill, made famous by the eponymous film, it is, essentially, a biscuit boutique and icing café, but it is also a charming place to book for a delicious, fun afternoon tea. Think about Biscuiteers if you are planning a visit to Portobello Road, whose world-famous street market has stalls offering everything from fruit and bread to posters, vintage clothes, ceramics, and music.

Everything is served on jolly red-and-white-striped pottery, is freshly prepared on the premises, and is quintessentially British.

ADDRESS: 194 Kensington Park Road, Notting Hill, London W11 2ES

TEL: +44 (0)20 7727 8096

EMAIL: nottinghill@biscuiteers.com

WEB: www.biscuiteers.com

AFTERNOON TEA SERVED: Monday to Saturday 10.30am–4.00pm, Sunday 11.30am–4.00pm. Pre-booking advised, one week in advance, although some last-minute requests are possible.

SET TEAS: London Afternoon Tea, to which you can add a fun biscuit icing session. Vegetarian and gluten free menus available to order.

NEAREST UNDERGROUND STATIONS: Ladbroke Grove, Westbourne Park

PLACES OF INTEREST NEARBY: Portobello Road, Notting Hill

Fresh-as-a-daisy finger sandwiches and good fruit scones with jam and clotted cream are accompanied by an array of cakes and patisserie. Biscuiteers' loyal customers were asked to vote for their favourite pastries to be served with the afternoon tea, and your cake stand has an array of miniature versions of these, including, amongst many others, a tiny Bakewell tart, a salted caramel brownie (to die for), and an individual traditional Victoria sponge. You'll also have hand-piped macarons and, of course, a selection of Biscuiteers iconic iced biscuits, resplendent with a London theme. Enjoy a good strong cuppa to go with the food, and take home anything you can't eat packed in one of the shop's charming boxes. It will be surprising if you manage to leave without buying any of the myriad of iced biscuits for which the shop is famous. And if you want to add a bit of fun to your afternoon tea, why not get creative and book an additional DIY biscuit icing session? Then you'll have even more to take home and enjoy later on.

THE BLOOMSBURY

Dalloway Terrace

*J*ust a stroll from the British Museum, and in the heart of Bloomsbury, Dalloway Terrace at the Bloomsbury Hotel is a lovely place to enjoy a traditional afternoon tea. The terrace is named in honour of Virginia Woolf and her best-known novel, *Mrs Dalloway*, which was published in 1925 whilst the author was living nearby at 52 Tavistock Square. Inside, the hotel itself is evocative of the era when Woolf and her fellow artists and writers, all members of the 'Bloomsbury Set', lived and worked in the area.

The inside-outside terrace is like being out-of-doors, but without the risks. It's an all-seasons terrace, serving all-day food as well as afternoon tea, and is lush with greenery, warmed by the sun in summer, fully protected from rain, and equipped with heaters and lovely, cosy rugs for cooler days. Come Christmas, it gets transformed into

ADDRESS: 16–22 Great Russell
Street, Bloomsbury, London
WC1B 3NN

TEL: +44 (0)20 7347 1221

EMAIL: info@dallowayterrace.com

WEB: www.dallowayterrace.com

OFFERS: see www.afternoontea
.co.uk/uk/london

AFTERNOON TEA SERVED:
daily 12.00pm–4.00pm

SET TEAS: traditional, with
sparkling and champagne options.
Seasonal special menus available.

**NEAREST UNDERGROUND
STATIONS:** Tottenham
Court Road

**PLACES OF INTEREST
NEARBY:** British Museum,
Oxford Street, Charing Cross Road,
Cartoon Museum

a winter wonderland. Given that you are not
far from the bustle of Oxford Street, this is an
oasis of calm in the heart of London, and a
very good place to rest awhile.

Your tiered cake stand is delivered with four
kinds of sandwiches, each on a different artisan
bread. Think tomato, beetroot, 'pain de mie',
and multigrain, and by all means ask for more.
Freshly baked buttermilk scones served with
clotted cream and homemade preserves follow,
and then come the sweet treats, with a nice
mix of patisserie and miniature cakes to tickle
the taste buds. Rare Tea Company supplies the
leaf tea here, with something to suit everyone,
from black, white, and green teas to caffeine-
free herbal infusions. The lemon verbena from
Provence makes a wonderful digestive, whilst
the second flush Muscatel Darjeeling is highly
fragrant with a heady floral aroma and soft
notes of muscatel grapes.

BRIGIT'S BAKERY

*B*rigit's Bakery, or B Bakery, is a heavenly place to escape the bustle of Covent Garden and The Strand. Essentially a French salon de thé, it is as pretty as a picture, very comfortable, and oh so chic. If you are seated on the ground floor, you can watch the world go by, but for some privacy, there is seating downstairs, and private rooms are also available for parties. You do need to order the set tea in advance, but can drop in anytime for a pot of tea and a scone or a cake. Tea is served on an eclectic mix of mismatched bone china cup, saucers, and plates. The tiered cake stands come laden with delicious savouries and sandwiches, all with a French twist, and the dainty cakes and pastries are a delight. Super scones with jam and cream complete the treat, and you definitely won't leave hungry

ADDRESS: 6–7 Chandos Place, Covent Garden, London WC2N 4HU

TEL: +44 (0)20 3026 1188

EMAIL: info@b-bakery.com

WEB: www.b-bakery.com

AFTERNOON TEA SERVED: Monday to Friday 11.00am–5.00pm, Saturday 11.00am–6.00pm, Sunday 11.00am–5.00pm

SET TEAS: traditional, Christmas. Book at least 24 hours in advance, and specify any dietary requirements. Gluten free, vegetarian, and halal available to pre-order when booking. Extensive à la carte menu available.

NEAREST UNDERGROUND STATIONS: Covent Garden, Charing Cross (and mainline trains)

PLACES OF INTEREST NEARBY: Covent Garden, London Transport Museum, Sir John Soane's Museum

BRIGIT'S BAKERY AFTERNOON TEA BUS AND BOAT TOURS

There can hardly be a more unique way to treat yourself to afternoon tea than by combining it with a sightseeing tour around the capital. With Brigit's Bakery, you can choose a bus ride or a cruise along the River Thames. Evocative of Swinging London, Brigit's 1960s Red Routemaster London buses have been refurbished and decked out with comfy banquet seating and shiny white tables and garlanded with flowers, albeit artificial ones. You'll have a uniformed driver ready to take you on an hour and a half's magical tour of London, whilst lovely staff serve you your afternoon tea and add interest to the event. Unless you are too engrossed in eating, you'll have the opportunity to take in many of London's famous landmarks, from Big Ben, Buckingham Palace, the London Eye, and Downing Street to Piccadilly, Knightsbridge, and the Royal Albert Hall. For safety reasons, your tea can't be served in a china cup, but you'll get a lovely Brigit's Bakery heatproof mug, which also serves as a souvenir of the event. The food is as fresh as a daisy and delicious, from the tiny savoury quiches, the finger sandwiches, and the mini baguettes to the exquisite

Bus Tours (all year)

TEL: +44 (0)20 3026 1188

EMAIL: bus@b-bakery.com

WEB: www.b-bakery.com

OPTION A: Pick-up at 8 Northumberland Avenue (near Trafalgar Square), Westminster, London WC2N 5BY

TOUR TIME DEPARTURES: daily at 12.30pm and 3.00pm

NEAREST UNDERGROUND STATIONS: Charing Cross

OPTION B: Pick-up at Victoria Coach Station, 164 Buckingham Palace Road, Belgravia, London SW1W 9TP (your booking confirmation will provide details of the exact gate location)

TOUR TIME DEPARTURES: daily at 12.00pm, 1.00pm, 2.30pm, 3.30pm, and 5.30pm

NEAREST UNDERGROUND STATIONS: Victoria

SET TEAS: traditional, gluten free, vegetarian, and halal available to pre-order when booking. Gin Lovers bus tours on selected dates.

patisserie, which might include a dainty fairy cake, a petit choux à la crème, a macaron, and a delicate seasonal fruit tartelette in the crispiest of pastry. As befits a traditional afternoon tea, there are warm scones, jam, and clotted cream. What a wonderful and entertaining experience this is.

As for the boat tours, on a few selected dates in the summer you can take in the sights and sounds of London as you sail along the mighty River Thames on a refurbished 1980s vintage private motor yacht. The cruise starts at 2.00pm from Butler's Wharf Pier, near London Bridge, and lasts around two and a half hours. It gets underway with a glass of champagne on the deck, giving you the opportunity to take in some breathtaking views of the capital. The lovely afternoon tea is served below deck in the dining room by the friendly uniformed staff. The afternoon tea is a treat of sandwiches, mini quiches, tiny cupcakes, scones, macarons, and more. Depending on how many people are in your party, you may be sharing a table. A truly memorable event.

Boat Tours (selected summer dates only)

TEL: +44 (0)20 3026 1188

EMAIL: boat@b-bakery.com

WEB: http://london.b-bakery.com/afternoon-tea/afternoon-tea-boat-tour

SET TEAS: traditional, gluten free, vegetarian, and halal available to pre-order when booking

BROWN'S HOTEL
The English Tea Room

*Q*uintessentially English, Brown's began life as four adjacent Georgian houses before Lord Byron's butler and his wife, who was Lady Byron's maid, created a hotel here in 1837. Tea has been served here ever since, and more than 170 years on, you would find it hard to surpass the surroundings and ambience of the English Tea Room, where the staff are dedicated to the highest level of service and take care of guests with the utmost courtesy and discreet efficiency. The elegant room is a harmonious combination of contemporary furnishings and artwork, original wood paneling, and antique fireplaces where open fires glow in the colder months. The tables are set with crisp linen and fine bone china, and the pianist playing gently in the background creates a lovely atmosphere.

ADDRESS: 33 Albemarle Street, Mayfair, London W1S 4BP

TEL: +44 (0)20 7518 4155

EMAIL: tea.browns@roccofortehotels.com

WEB: www.roccofortehotels.com

OFFERS: see www.afternoontea .co.uk/uk/london

AFTERNOON TEA SERVED: daily bookings at 12.00pm, 12.30pm, 2.30pm, 3.00pm, 5.30pm. Booking advisable.

SET TEAS: traditional, champagne or rosé champagne, Tea-Tox Healthy or Tea-Tox Healthy Champagne Afternoon Tea, festive and seasonal teas. Gluten-free option available, but please give 48 hours' notice.

DRESS CODE: smart casual; trainers/sneakers, t-shirts, shorts, and sportswear are not permitted

NEAREST UNDERGROUND STATIONS: Piccadilly Circus, Green Park

PLACES OF INTEREST NEARBY: Royal Academy of Arts, Burlington Arcade, Green Park, St James's Park, Bond Street, Cork Street art galleries, Savile Row, Fortnum & Mason

The traditional tea features all the important ingredients, from extremely good finger sandwiches on a variety of breads, to super fruit and plain scones served with clotted cream and strawberry jam. You'll welcome the palate cleanser that precedes the daintiest of pastries, which, depending on the season, could include a delectable peach and lemon verbena macaron, a violet and berry cheesecake, or a pistachio and cherry financier. If you are watching your waistline and looking for a healthier option, then Tea-Tox, created by Madeleine Shaw, is just the ticket. There are no scones served with this tea, but rather imaginative open sandwiches and savouries, a platter of fresh fruit with yogurt and honey, and sugarless cakes and desserts. There is even a low-calorie champagne. Regardless of the tea you choose, expect everything to be regularly replenished and for your teapot to be refilled with the finest loose-leaf tea chosen from over seventeen listed in the Tea Library, including two of Brown's own special blends. An hour and a half whiled away in the English Tea Room will refresh and revive you, and as you leave there is a gift of cake to take home with you. Brown's Hotel is, justifiably, a very popular haunt for visitors and locals alike, so be sure to book in advance.

CLARIDGE'S

The Foyer and Reading Room

*A*rt deco fans will be in seventh heaven at Claridge's, for it is a jewel of a hotel, and a complex architectural masterpiece. The hotel has evolved over the years from the original Victorian building, designed by C W Stephens in 1896, and the addition of Oswald Milne's art deco ballroom wing in 1929. His talents, combined with those of designer Basil Ionides and other art deco artists in the 1920s and 30s, created this iconic building, with possibly the most glamorous hotel entrance in London. Crossing the threshold into the foyer, you will be dazzled by the magnificent silver-white light sculpture from Seattle-based artist Dale Chihuly, which hangs from the eighteen-foot-high ceiling. Made up of over 800 individually hand-blown and sculpted pieces of glass, it is both spectacular and a definite talking point.

By contrast, the adjoining Reading Room, with its comfortable leather banquettes, elegant mirrors, suede walls, and cut marble fireplaces, is a more intimate space in

ADDRESS: Brook Street, Mayfair, London W1A 2JQ

TEL: +44 (0)20 7107 8872

EMAIL: dining@claridges.co.uk

WEB: www.claridges.co.uk

AFTERNOON TEA SERVED: daily at 2.45pm, 3.00pm, 3.15pm, 3.30pm, 4.45pm, 5.00pm, 5.15pm, 5.30pm. Bookings taken up to three months in advance.

SET TEAS: traditional, various champagne teas including Rosé and Vintage Champagne, Children's Afternoon Tea, themed teas including Valentine's Afternoon Tea, Chelsea Flower Show Afternoon Tea, Great British Afternoon Tea. Gluten free available with notice.

DRESS CODE: elegant smart casual; no shorts, vests, sportswear, flip-flops, ripped jeans, or baseball caps

NEAREST UNDERGROUND STATIONS: Bond Street

PLACES OF INTEREST NEARBY: Wallace Collection, Bond Street, Regent Street, Green Park, Hyde Park

which to enjoy the sophisticated, award-winning afternoon tea of which Claridge's is justly proud. What an experience it is to have your tea presented to you on beautiful Bernardaud green and white porcelain by the impeccably-suited staff. The food is fit for royalty and is unusual without being pretentious. The set afternoon tea is designed to soothe and revive the heartiest shopper or guest; a selection of sandwiches is complemented by the most delightful raisin and apple scones, served, of course, with thick Cornish clotted cream and the hotel's own popular Marco Polo jelly. Make sure you leave some room for the exquisite French pastries that follow. The selection changes daily and might include chocolate roulade, strawberry tartlets, or vanilla mille-feuille. The choices don't end here, for besides the champagnes on offer, there are 30 different varieties of tea, carefully sourced from all over the world by the hotel's tea connoisseur, Henrietta Lovell, and

selected to perfectly complement the food. Whenever you visit Claridge's for tea, there will be a pianist and violinist playing soothing music, so sit back, relax, and revel in the ultimate tea experience.

CLIVEDEN HOUSE

liveden House, built in 1666 by the 2nd Duke of Buckingham as a gift for his mistress, has a vivid and intriguing history and must be one of the oldest stately homes in the country where hotel guests can indulge in a quintessentially English afternoon tea. The house, which has hosted every British monarch since George I, was bought by William Waldorf Astor in 1893, and during the First World War, several of the estate's buildings served as a Red Cross hospital. Post-war, Cliveden became a mecca for the rich and famous, and hosted visitors including President Roosevelt, Charlie Chaplin, and George Bernard-Shaw, amongst others. And it was here, in 1963, alongside Bill Astor's new outdoor swimming pool, that John Profumo, the secretary of state for war, met call girl Christine Keeler,

ADDRESS: Cliveden Road, Taplow, Berkshire SL6 0JF

TEL: +44 (0)1628 668 561

EMAIL: reservations@clivedenhouse.co.uk

WEB: www.clivedenhouse.co.uk /dine-with-us/afternoon-tea

AFTERNOON TEA SERVED: Monday to Friday 2.30pm—4.30pm

SET TEAS: Cliveden Traditional, Cliveden Champagne Afternoon Tea, Cliveden '66 Traditional Afternoon Tea

NEAREST MAINLINE STATIONS: Taplow, Burnham, Slough

PLACES OF INTEREST NEARBY: National Trust grounds, Stanley Spencer Gallery at Cookham, Bekonscot Model Village, Henley, Cliveden Boathouse for a Thames cruise on a Vintage Launch, Legoland Windsor, Windsor Castle, Boulter's Lock and Ray Mill Island

igniting the biggest scandal British politics had ever known and almost bringing down the government. From private house to university premises, Cliveden finally became an iconic Grade 1 listed hotel in 1985.

This is a truly grand country house, and brings to mind images of Downton Abbey and a bygone era. The staff go out of their way to make you feel welcome and are most attentive. Tea is generally served in the Great Hall, resplendent with oak-panelled walls and ceiling, priceless artworks, antique furniture, and even a few suits of armor. If you visit in the winter months, there will be a fire roaring in the grand fireplace.

Afternoon tea here is all about excellent service and attention to detail, and is truly traditional, from the finger sandwiches and the savoury cheese and dill scone topped with a piped smoked salmon mousse, to the dainty fruit and plain scones, served with excellent strawberry jam and clotted cream. Taking into account seasonal changes, the sweet course will have an éclair, an individual dark chocolate popcorn cake, and several other bite-sized delicacies. You can indulge as much as you like with refills of everything, and take as long as you want over your tea. A small, select tea list includes the robust Cliveden Blend, Lapsang

Souchong Imperial, and Earl Grey Extra. The ribbon design on the William Edwards fine bone china is based on the original that was commissioned especially for Lady Astor, and if you would like a lasting memento of your visit, you can purchase a tea set for two of this fabulous tea service.

No trip to Cliveden would be complete without a stroll around the 376-acre estate, which is owned, managed, and cared for by the National Trust. Here you can see some wonderful art installations, challenge your sense of direction in the maze, and visit the amphitheatre where the first recital of 'Rule Brittania' was played. What a way to end the day.

THE CONNAUGHT

Jean-Georges

The Connaught Hotel is to be found in a quiet corner in the heart of Mayfair village, just off Berkeley Square. Afternoon tea here is an elegant occasion, taken in the stylish surroundings of the restaurant in the conservatory extension. Named after the world-renowned chef Jean-Georges Vongerichten, the redesigned room is a beautiful, light, bright, and very comfortable space that curves around the hotel from Mount Street to Carlos Place. The wall-to-ceiling windows, accented with vibrant stained glass panels which catch the changing light, give you a clear view of 'Silence', the mystical fountain on the street outside, created by Japanese architect Tadao Ando.

ADDRESS: Carlos Place, Mayfair, London W1K 2AL

TEL: +44 (0)20 7107 8861

EMAIL: jeangeorges@the-connaught.co.uk

WEB: www.the-connaught.co.uk

AFTERNOON TEA SERVED: daily at 2.30pm and 4.30pm. Dietary requirements can be catered for with advance notice.

SET TEAS: traditional afternoon tea and champagne option

NEAREST UNDERGROUND STATIONS: Bond Street, Green Park

PLACES OF INTEREST NEARBY: Mayfair Village, Balenciaga and Marc Jacobs flagship stores, Gagosian Gallery, Dunhill's Bourdon House, Bond Street, Marylebone High Street

Jean-Georges is the perfect place to sit and relax while you watch the world go by and let the charming staff take care of you. Everything is explained to you, and your tea begins with a melt-in-the-mouth savoury amuse-bouche, accompanied by an optional glass of champagne. The finger sandwiches that follow have classic fillings transformed by Jean-Georges' witty twist. Take the smoked salmon, which is given a kick with Mexican chili, chipotle, coriander, and spring onions, or the mustard, honey, and walnuts that perfectly partner the ham and aged cheese sandwich. Then there is the all-time favourite cucumber sandwich, which is jazzed up with Greek yogurt, a twist of lime, and a hint of mint. The plain and raisin scones are light, fluffy, and delicious, especially with the addition of a zingy lemon curd, homemade strawberry jam, and clotted cream.

Start the final sweet course with the miniature chocolate fondue, and, depending on the season, dip strawberries or ginger cake into the rich chocolate liquid. The dainty, exquisitely crafted pastries, including a hugely popular Rocher of hazelnut praline and milk chocolate,

are the crowning glory to a first-rate feast. Of course, all this is accompanied by an excellent cup of tea. There's a good choice from Mariage Frères, including French breakfast tea, an elegant and refined, full-bodied blend; Darjeeling Beauty, a rare vintage for connoisseurs; Thé à L'Opéra; Gyokuro Earl Grey French; and Ceylon Orange Pekoe. Besides these, and more, there is a selection of fresh teas which change with the seasons. Afternoon tea is the most English of celebrations, and the Connaught's offering is amongst the very best.

CONRAD LONDON ST JAMES
Emmeline's Lounge

*L*ocated in the heart of historic St James and Westminster, Emmeline's at Conrad London St James is situated within an historic late 19th-century building that was once Queen Anne's Chamber. Tenants have included barristers who needed to be near the Houses of Parliament, the Brewers' Society, and, during the Second World War, it served as a wartime residence for lobbyists and civil servants. Behind the façade you'll find a transformed building with a stunning light-filled entrance hall and lobby, quirky original art installations, wonderful floral arrangements, and, for afternoon tea takers, Emmeline's Lounge. Being so close to the Houses of Parliament, it's fitting to name the lounge in memory of Emmeline Pankhurst, the 19th-century British political activist and founder of the militant Women's Social and Political Union, who fought for the vote for women.

You'll be very much at home here, seated in comfortable chairs at beautifully set tables in a room that is understatedly luxurious. The staff are most attentive and

ADDRESS: 22–28 Broadway, Westminster, London SW1H 0BH

TEL: +44 (0)20 3301 1400

EMAIL: tea@conradstjames.com

WEB: www.conradhotels3.hilton.com

AFTERNOON TEA SERVED: daily 1.30pm–6.00pm. Jazz afternoon tea on Saturdays.

SET TEAS: seasonally changing afternoon tea, free-flowing champagne option, special event teas including Christmas, Mother's Day, Halloween. Gluten-free and most dietary requirements can be accommodated, preferably with advance booking. Special price for children aged 10 years and under.

NEAREST UNDERGROUND STATIONS: St James's Park

PLACES OF INTEREST NEARBY: Buckingham Palace, Big Ben, Westminster Abbey, Westminster Hall, Houses of Parliament, St James's Park, Royal Courts of Justice, New Scotland Yard

knowledgeable and go out of their way to make your visit memorable. Afternoon tea starts off with a selection of savouries; depending on the season, this might be a miniature heritage tomato and red onion tart with basil accompanied by a prawn and crab Bloody Mary. Moving on to the five varieties of sandwiches, each is served on a different artisan bread and is more delicious than the one before. Refills are there if you can manage them, but remember there are scones, pastries, and cakes to follow. Smashing fruit and plain scones are served with strawberry compote, lemon curd, and Devonshire clotted cream, which brings you on to the sweet treats. Again, these change to reflect the seasons, so in the summer you might have, amongst other delights, a shot glass filled with a Pimm's trifle and a raspberry and pistachio choux bun. There are more than two bites to the mini cakes, which could be chocolate or yummy almond and apricot. Take home what you can't manage in a customised box. There is a free-flowing champagne option if you feel like splurging a bit, and if you visit on a Saturday, you'll have live music to entertain you. The afternoon tea here is of an excellent quality and remarkably good value.

CORINTHIA HOTEL
The Crystal Moon Lounge

*G*o through the grand entrance of this historic building, across the lobby, and up the stairs into the Crystal Moon Lounge, and you arrive at the very heart of the luxurious Corinthia, a wonderful space where you can indulge in afternoon tea. Understated elegance prevails, natural light floods in from the glass-domed ceiling onto the fabulous Baccarat glass chandelier, and exotic flowers adorn the central table. Of all the spaces in the hotel, the Crystal Moon Lounge is probably the most glamorous, and here you are seated in a comfortable armchair at a table set with fine linen and bespoke bone china designed by William Edwards. On a warm day, you can take your tea outside in an alfresco setting.

Afternoon tea here is so much more than a traditional feast, and begins with selecting your tea. On offer is a vast selection of black, green, and white loose-leaf

ADDRESS: Whitehall Place, Westminster, London SW1A 2BD

TEL: +44 (0)20 7321 3150

EMAIL: restaurants.london@corinthia.com

WEB: www.corinthia.com/en/hotels /london/dining/afternoon-tea

AFTERNOON TEA SERVED: Monday to Friday 2.00pm–6.00pm, Saturday and Sunday 12.00pm–6.00pm

SET TEAS: traditional afternoon tea, seasonal menus, and celebratory teas. Vegetarian and other options available on request.

NEAREST UNDERGROUND STATIONS: Embankment

PLACES OF INTEREST NEARBY: National Gallery, National Portrait Gallery, South Bank, Thames Embankment, Whitehall, 10 Downing Street, London Eye

teas, including the hotel's own unique blend, Corinthia Signature English Breakfast, which combines a rich, intense, malty Assam with a more mellow Ceylon Orange Pekoe and a mild Keemun. Teas are supplied by Camellia's Tea House, and include a variety of flavoured, herbal, and fruit teas, so there is something to suit every palate. There are trained tea sommeliers on hand who will guide you through the selection before you opt for your flavour of choice.

For the food, you will start with an amuse-bouche, followed by finger sandwiches made using interesting breads with mouth-watering fillings. You'll be served assorted scones that are crisp on the outside and light inside, complemented by handmade preserves, clotted cream, and lemon curd. The English tea fancies are the finishing touch, and are picture perfect and delicious. Depending on the season, these might include a Baba Surprise, a Tahitian vanilla and rhubarb tartlet with Tonka bean cream, and a salted caramel delight. Everything will be replenished if you so desire. Besides the set afternoon tea, the Lobby Table has an array of glass-domed cake stands which

display a selection of traditional afternoon tea cakes and tarts. These change on a daily basis and are not included in the set menu. For an extra special treat, add a glass of Laurent-Perrier Champagne, or celebrate with a glass of Rosé Champagne. And if you are looking to celebrate Easter, Mother's Day, the Chelsea Flower Show, Wimbledon, Halloween, or Christmas, then the Corinthia London has a seasonal tea to fit the occasion. Regardless of when you visit, the lovely food and drink, along with the thoughtful and attentive service, make this a delightful experience.

COWORTH PARK
The Drawing Room

*I*n the best of 18th-century English houses, the drawing room was traditionally reserved for entertaining guests after dinner. This changed once Anna, the 7th Duchess of Bedford, began inviting her friends to join her for a pot of tea and light refreshments, and it soon became the favoured venue for afternoon tea. Today, any duchess would feel at home enjoying afternoon tea in the drawing room or the adjoining conservatory of the mansion house at Coworth Park. The surroundings are elegant and the views across the hotel's terraces, meadows, and the beautiful Berkshire countryside are stunning. The room is filled with luxury sofas and fabrics, specially commissioned chandeliers, and artwork. This is all complemented by

ADDRESS: Blacknest Road, Ascot, Berkshire SL5 7SE

TEL: +44 (0)1344 876 600

EMAIL: info.cpa@dorchestercollection.com

WEB: www.dorchestercollection .com/en/ascot/coworth-park

AFTERNOON TEA SERVED: Drawing Room, Monday to Thursday 12.30pm–5.30pm; Friday to Sunday, first sitting 2.30pm–4.15pm, second sitting 4.45pm–6.30pm. Spatisserie, 2.30pm–5.30pm.

SET TEAS: traditional afternoon tea with seasonal variations, children's tea, special teas for Mother's Day, Valentine's Day, and other occasions. Gluten-free option available.

NEAREST MAINLINE STATIONS: Sunningdale, Virginia Water

PLACES OF INTEREST NEARBY: Ascot Racecourse, Guards Polo Academy, Coworth Park Equestrian Centre, Windsor Castle, Windsor Great Park

the beautiful marble fireplaces at either end of the room, which contain a mosaic of decorative Wedgwood and Spode porcelain fragments.

As one would expect from a hotel of this calibre, the afternoon tea is very good indeed, and offers a twist on the traditional. The menus alter to reflect the seasonally changing landscape of Coworth Park's 240 acres of picturesque parkland. In summer, enjoy the Meadow afternoon tea, followed by the Orchard menu in the autumn, a glorious festive tea over the winter and Christmas time, and a traditional tea which reappears in spring. The food here is of the highest standard: excellent sandwiches refilled as often as you want, good scones with the essential accompaniment of preserves and clotted cream, and delicate pastries and desserts inspired by the garden. Depending on the time of year, you might enjoy a summer trifle with strawberries and elderflower, a raspberry and meadowsweet frangipane tart, or the marmalade cake, a classic sponge with homemade Coworth Park marmalade topped with cardamom cream. Ask for any you wish to be replenished, and take

home any leftovers. On Saturday and Sunday afternoons, you can enjoy afternoon tea accompanied by live music from the hotel's harpist.

The tea list in the drawing room includes over twenty varieties, amongst them Coworth Park's own Meadow Blend, which contains lavender picked from the hotel's grounds. There are fine teas, including the rare Silver Needles, and the British heritage teas feature Coworth Park Afternoon Blend and Original English Breakfast. You don't need to miss out on afternoon tea if you are taking advantage of the beautiful spa at Coworth Park, for the same delicious fare, albeit with a smaller list of leaf tea, is served in the glorious Spatisserie. And remember, if you possibly can, to have a stroll in the glorious gardens before you leave.

DEAN STREET TOWNHOUSE

The Dean Street Townhouse, converted from two adjoining four-storey Georgian properties, has a character and atmosphere all of its own that is quirky, lively, and subtly stylish. Originally built in the 1730s, the houses were home to a variety of people, from aristocrats to musical publishers to Soho luminaries. Most famously, the rooftop of 69 Dean Street was home to the Gargoyle Club, founded in 1925, an establishment which became the 'in' place for London society and which was the epitome of decadent glamour. If you think of past members, including Fred Astaire, Noël Coward, and artists Francis Bacon and Lucien Freud, you can get an idea of the atmosphere and ambience. Since Dean Street Townhouse opened in 2009, it has earned a reputation as a cool hotel, and is beloved of Soho socialites, film buffs, and tourists alike.

ADDRESS: 69–71 Dean Street, Soho, London W1D 3SE

TEL: +44 (0)20 7434 1775

WEB: www.deanstreettownhouse.com

AFTERNOON TEA SERVED: daily 2.00pm–6.00pm

SET TEAS: cream tea, traditional tea, champagne tea, with high tea options, including vegetarian items

NEAREST UNDERGROUND STATIONS: Tottenham Court Road

PLACES OF INTEREST NEARBY: Theatreland, Soho, Leicester Square, Chinatown

Now you can take a truly English tea in the restaurant area with its stripped wood flooring, half-panelled walls, red leather banquettes, and upholstered chairs, and gaze at the contemporary art collection including works by Peter Blake, Tracey Emin, and others. Alternatively, you can sit and people-watch from your comfy armchair looking out onto Dean Street, or cosy up in similar comfort in The Parlour in front of a roaring fire on a chilly day. Blue Burleigh crockery adds to the old-fashioned feel of the place, and eager young staff will serve you a jolly good feast. You may find it hard to resist adding some buttery crumpets to your order, or, if it's getting late in the day, an old-fashioned savoury delight such as macaroni cheese or yummy welsh rarebit, not to mention fish fingers, a sausage roll, or Scotch duck egg. This is the nicest of places to relax and have a wonderfully comforting afternoon tea.

THE DORCHESTER

The Promenade

*T*he Promenade is at the heart of The Dorchester, and afternoon tea here ranks amongst the very best that London has to offer. The hotel has the accolade of having served afternoon tea to guests for over eighty-five years, and this experience is evident wherever you look. From the moment you cross the threshold of this stunning venue, with its luxurious and elegant décor, magnificent floral arrangements, and series of warm, intimate seating areas, you can be certain of enjoying an indulgent afternoon tea. The ambience is relaxed, the service impeccable, and no detail has been overlooked. The tables are set with crisp linen tablecloths, beautiful silver-edged bone china, and glorious fresh flowers, and the resident pianist provides an unobtrusive backdrop.

The Dorchester's traditional afternoon tea menu has all the elements you would expect, beginning with the presentation of a palate-cleansing 'Flowering Tea.' The flowering process takes long enough for you to enjoy a glass of champagne before you are served a selection of finger sandwiches on a variety of artisan breads. Some

ADDRESS: 53 Park Lane, Mayfair, London W1K 1QA

TEL: +44 (0)20 7629 8888

EMAIL: restaurant@thedorchester.com

WEB: www.thedorchester.com /afternoon-tea

OFFERS: see www.afternoontea .co.uk/uk/london

AFTERNOON TEA SERVED:
The Promenade, Monday to Thursday, six sittings: 1.00pm, 1.30pm, 3.15pm, 3.45pm, 5.30pm, 6.00pm; Friday to Sunday, five sittings: 1.00pm, 2.00pm, 3.15pm, 4.30pm, 5.30pm. The Spatisserie, daily, three sittings: 1.00pm, 1.30pm, 2.00pm.

more of the flowering tea will leave you ready to enjoy the sweet courses to the maximum. The delectable warm raisin and plain scones are served with homemade strawberry jam, a seasonal jam, and Cornish clotted cream, and are followed by a sublime selection of floral-inspired dainty French pastries, which change with the seasons. When it comes to Christmas, the Dorchester celebrates in style; every weekend from mid-November until Christmas Eve, you can share in the occasion with their Christmas Carols afternoon tea, drinking a glass of champagne whilst you listen to the children's school choir as they sing all the festive favourites.

As you would expect from a venue of this calibre, the Dorchester tea menu is top rate, and includes many rare varieties. Two Dalreoch teas from the Highlands of Scotland are high up the list, having won top honours at the Salon de Thé awards in Paris. There are

three Dorchester blends: Breakfast, which combines silvery Ceylon with golden Assam; Afternoon, a blend of single estate teas from Sri Lanka and Assam; and a seasonal flower blend, perfectly complementing the flower arrangements and tea pastries. Special seasonal teas include Darjeeling First Flush and Assam Second Flush, and amongst the rare and limited offerings are the highly prized Silver Dawn and Golden Tips. The list goes on and on with black, green, white, oolong, natural, flavoured, and caffeine-free infusions.

If you happen to be treating yourself to a visit to the Spatisserie, then you can enjoy the Promenade afternoon tea menus in the calm and intimate surroundings of the opulent spa. It is hardly surprising that guests are as reluctant to leave The Dorchester as they are eager to arrive.

SET TEAS: traditional, champagne with a choice of three, including a Dom Pérignon Vintage. See the website for seasonal and themed teas, which include Easter, Chelsea Flower Show, Wimbledon, and Christmas teas. Vegan, vegetarian, and gluten-free menus available on request, preferably in advance.

DRESS CODE: smart casual; no baseball caps, beanie hats, ripped jeans, sportswear, trainers/sneakers, flip-flops, or shorts

NEAREST UNDERGROUND STATIONS: Hyde Park Corner, Marble Arch

PLACES OF INTEREST NEARBY: Apsley House, Buckingham Palace, Albert Memorial, Hyde Park, Victoria and Albert Museum, Knightsbridge, Bond Street

EGERTON HOUSE HOTEL

*T*he elegant drawing room at Egerton House, which is made up of a pair of Victorian townhouses, is one of the Red Carnation boutique hotel collection, and is the perfect place for a very enjoyable, relaxing afternoon tea. If you are a dog lover, this is just the place to go, for you can take your pooch – small or large – along and let them enjoy their own special treat. Whilst your dog is busy enjoying the homemade chicken and beef meatloaf, the doggy biscuit, and, believe it or not, doggylicious ice cream, you will be tucking into a jolly good tea that showcases favourite traditional British cakes.

First things first, though: you'll start with the sandwiches, which are presented on a variety of interesting breads. The Cape seed loaf used for the smoked salmon is made using Red Carnation president and founder Bea Tollman's own recipe, and is delicious, as are the round egg mayonnaise sandwiches rolled in flaked almonds. It's a nice change to have cucumber and cream cheese served on sundried tomato bread, and

ADDRESS: 17–19 Egerton Terrace, London SW3 2BX

TEL: +44 (0)20 7589 2412

EMAIL: bookeg@rchmail.com

WEB: www.egertonhousehotel.com

AFTERNOON TEA SERVED: daily 12.00pm–6.00pm

SET TEAS: cream tea, Great British Afternoon Tea, champagne tea, Teddy Bear's Picnic with Edwin (for under 12 years old, 24 hours' notice required), Doggy Afternoon Tea, vegan, vegetarian, gluten free, picnics. Pre-booking advised for all teas.

NEAREST UNDERGROUND STATIONS: Knightsbridge

PLACES OF INTEREST NEARBY: Harrods, Hyde Park, Brompton Oratory, Victoria and Albert Museum, Royal Albert Hall

the coronation chicken on granary bread makes an equally good combination. Before you tackle the fruit and plain scones, remember to leave room for the selection of homemade cakes and the individual trifle waiting for you on the top tier. There is Battenberg cake, Victoria sponge, lemon drizzle cake, and an individual Bakewell tart, and it is a struggle to eat them all. Not to worry, though, as you can take home any uneaten treats, whilst your pet pooch will leave with a special chew toy. Egerton House is happy to arrange all sorts of afternoon tea parties, including doggy birthday parties.

Cape Seed Loaf

Recipe courtesy of Egerton House Hotel

INGREDIENTS

- 420 g (4¼ cups) whole wheat flour
- 82 g (¾ cup) plain (all-purpose) flour
- 62 g (½ cup + 2 Tbsp.) muesli
- 65 g (½ cup) raisins
- 20 g (1 Tbsp. + 1 tsp.) baking soda
- 10 g (2 tsp.) salt
- 120 g (1 cup) walnut pieces
- 155 g (1 cup + 2 Tbsp.) pumpkin seeds
- 186 g (1¼ cups) flax seeds
- 166 g (1 cup + 3 Tbsp.) sunflower seeds
- 1.1 L (4 cups) plain yoghurt
- 125 g (½ cup + 2 Tbsp.) sunflower oil
- 75 g (¼ cup) runny (clear) honey
- 100 g (¾ cup) seeds for sprinkling on the tops of the loaves

Bea Tollman is President and Founder of the boutique Red Carnation Hotel Collection, which also includes The Milestone Hotel and The Rubens at the Palace. This recipe is from her cookbook *A Life in Food.* This bread freezes beautifully. Makes two loaves.

METHOD

1. Preheat the oven to 180ºC (350ºF).
2. Grease two loaf tins (pans) with a little butter and line the bottoms and sides with parchment paper.
3. In a large bowl, mix all of the dry ingredients together and set aside.
4. In a medium-size bowl, combine the yoghurt, oil, and honey and whisk until mixed thoroughly. Then, using a spatula, add the wet ingredients to the dry ingredients. Mix well (the bread mixture will be quite wet).
5. Divide the mixture between the two tins (pans) and sprinkle with the extra seeds. (This may seem like a lot of seeds, but many will fall off when you take the bread out of the tins/pans after baking.)
6. Bake in the centre of the oven for 1 hour. Remove breads from the tins (pans) and cool on a wire rack.

This recipe presents terms and measurements for both UK and US readers. Units are given first for UK readers in the original measurement units, then for US readers in converted units in parentheses. Do not mix the units. US equivalent terms are also given in parentheses where needed.

FORTNUM & MASON

*A*fternoon tea at Fortnum & Mason is a firmly established British tradition, and as you cross the threshold into the store, famed for its chiming clock, you get an inkling of the treat that awaits you upstairs. The ground floor resembles an exquisite Aladdin's cave, for it is filled with the most sublime displays of extraordinarily luxurious food, and with all the accessories needed to serve tea, from the unsurpassable range of leaf tea to silver tea strainers to fine bone china. Either walk up the red-carpeted stairs or take the brass-fixed and mirror-laden lift up to the fourth floor and the elegant and tranquil Diamond Jubilee Tea Salon. The salon, decorated throughout in calming eau-de-nil, was opened by Her Majesty the

ADDRESS: 181 Piccadilly, St James's, London W1A 1ER

TEL: +44 (0)20 7734 8040

EMAIL: reservations@fortnumandmason.co.uk

WEB: www.fortnumandmason.com /afternoontea.aspx

AFTERNOON TEA SERVED: Monday to Saturday 12.00pm–7.00pm, Sunday 12.00pm–6.00pm. Advance booking advised.

SET TEAS: Classic Afternoon Tea, Savoury Afternoon Tea, high tea, vegetarian, gluten free, dairy free, diabetic, egg allergy, vegan. Children's menu available.

NEAREST UNDERGROUND STATIONS: Green Park, Piccadilly

PLACES OF INTEREST NEARBY: Buckingham Palace, Royal Academy of Arts, Green Park, The Royal Institution

Queen in 2012, and is an iconic destination for the most traditional, refined afternoon tea.

The attentive service is legendary, there is a menu to suit every dietary requirement, and everything will be replenished as and when you like. For those choosing the quintessentially English tea, the feast of finger sandwiches has an array of tasty fillings, and the plain and fruit scones are rather good. Rest awhile before you tackle the individual patisserie on the cake tower, and then choose a slice of cake from the cake carriage to eat right away or to take home. You might prefer the savoury afternoon tea, which, besides the traditional sandwiches, offers a pea scone with smoked salmon cream cheese and a cheese and onion scone with grape jelly. Choose from the selection of savoury items, such as dressed crab on cucumber or smoked trout roulade with Keta caviar, and take home a treat from the cake carriage for later. For those wanting a more substantial feast, maybe pre-theatre, high tea is just the ticket. Comfort food eaten with great satisfaction includes Fortnum's famous Welsh Rarebit and a Lobster Omelette Victoria, followed by the scones, patisserie, and cake.

Tea was one of the first products that Fortnum & Mason sold nearly three centuries

ago, and they take the business of brewing extremely seriously. The choice of leaf is exceptional and unsurpassable, and their world-renowned expert 'Tearistas' are keen and eager to help and advise, and offer individual tea tastings at your table. Let them know what you like, or don't like, and the staff will come up with suggestions and encourage you to try something new. Guests may choose from a list of more than fifty teas, both blends and single-estate teas sourced from all over the globe; the list includes First Flush Tregothnan, the first truly English tea.

If you happen to be en route through St Pancras International Station, Fortnum's has established the perfect traveller's rest in the tea salon there. The tea menu is small but strong and includes an exclusive St Pancras blend, and there is plenty of opportunity to shop in this haven away from the bustle of an international station.

Also: Fortnum & Mason St Pancras Tea Salon

ADDRESS: The King's Cross St Pancras International Store can be approached via the lower level of St Pancras International; it is at the far end of the Arcade, opposite Eurostar Arrivals.

TEL: +44 (0)20 7734 8040

AFTERNOON TEA SERVED: daily from 11.00am

FOUR SEASONS HOTEL, PARK LANE

Amaranto Lounge

*W*hat better place to enjoy an exclusive afternoon tea which has been created to reflect the seasons of the year than the beautiful Four Seasons on Park Lane? The Amaranto Lounge has windows and mirrors galore and acres of marble, and is a perfect place to relax with its deep sofas and comfortable armchairs. The clean lines of the contemporary tiered cake stands are the perfect accompaniment for the delicately patterned fine Wedgwood china, worthy of the food served on it.

Excellent breads are used for the sandwich course, complemented with carefully selected fillings to suit all dietary requirements, and you'll be asked if you would like more of any sandwiches you choose. Traditional and raisin scones are just right in size

and texture. The jams, created especially for the Four Seasons by artisan makers Tea Together, always take advantage of a novel combination of the best seasonal fruits, and, with the addition of lemon curd and thick clotted cream, are a marriage made in heaven. For your sweet course, the executive pastry chef, David Oliver, has fashioned a selection of delectable seasonal pastries, like his summer creation of a delicate choux pastry picnic hamper, complete with basket weave, a chocolate cherry filling, and a 'gingham' tablecloth topping made of white chocolate. The inventiveness and delicacy has to be admired, and every morsel enjoyed. Your tea is from a list provided by Jing Tea, and includes the very rare Iron Buddha Oolong blend, Darjeeling First Flush, and Red Dragon, a unique and exceptional black tea blend. There are champagnes available as well as an alcohol-free rosé sparkling wine. Afternoon tea finishes with a slice of proper cake, which again makes the most of seasonal produce. One can look forward to tea here whatever the season of the year.

ADDRESS: Hamilton Place, Park Lane, Mayfair, London W1J 7DR

TEL: +44 (0)20 7319 5206

WEB: www.fourseasons.com/london

OFFERS: see www.afternoontea.co.uk/uk/london

AFTERNOON TEA SERVED: daily 1.30pm–6.00pm (last sitting 5.30pm)

SET TEAS: Traditional Seasonal Afternoon Tea, Vegetarian Seasonal Afternoon Tea

NEAREST UNDERGROUND STATIONS: Hyde Park Corner, Green Park

PLACES OF INTEREST NEARBY: Apsley House, Mayfair, Hyde Park

Lemon Cake

WITH RHUBARB AND VANILLA FILLING

Recipe courtesy of David Oliver at The Four Seasons Hotel, Park Lane

Lemon Cake

INGREDIENTS

- 125 g (1 cup) plain (all-purpose) flour
- 7 g (1¾ tsp.) baking powder
- 220 g (½ cup + 6 Tbsp.) butter, softened
- 220 g (1 cup) caster (superfine granulated) sugar
- Freshly grated zest of 2½ lemons
- 94 g (¾ cup) ground almonds
- 3 eggs (137 g/¾ cup)
- 60 g (¼ cup) milk
- 28 g (2 Tbsp.) butter

METHOD

1. Preheat the oven to 180°C (350°F).
2. Line the bottom and sides of a loaf tin (pan) with parchment (baking) paper.
3. Beat 3 eggs, then weigh the amount required.

*T*ry this interesting and flavorful cake the next time you are in the mood to bake. This recipe was created for a 900 g (2 lb.) loaf tin (pan).

This recipe presents terms and measurements for both UK and US readers. Units are given first for UK readers in the original measurement units, then for US readers in converted units in parentheses. Do not mix the units. US equivalent terms are also given in parentheses where needed.

4. Sift the flour and baking powder, then set aside.
5. In a medium-size bowl, combine the soft butter, sugar, lemon zest, and ground almonds. Beat until well combined and light in colour. Beat in the eggs a little at a time, mixing well. Add the flour and baking powder and mix until well combined. Add in the milk little by little, mixing well.
6. Pour the mixture into the prepared loaf tin (pan).
7. Melt about 28 g (1 oz.) of butter.
8. Dip a dough cutter or a straightedge utensil into the butter and then mark down the centre of the cake, pushing the utensil into the batter approximately 0.5 cm (¼ inch). This will allow the cake to split at the top as it rises and to regulate the shape for an attractive finish to the final cake.
9. Turn the oven down to 170°C (338°F) and bake for 30 minutes, then reduce to 160°C (320°F) and bake for an additional 30 to 40 minutes.
10. Insert a cake tester (skewer) into the centre of the cake. If it comes out clean, remove the cake from the oven; if not, continue baking for an additional 10 minutes.
11. Remove the cake from the tin (pan) and let cool on a wire rack. Once the cake has cooled, let it chill in the refrigerator for 2 hours. Then, using an apple corer, drill a hole all the way through the middle of the cake (lengthwise).

Rhubarb and Vanilla Compote

INGREDIENTS

- 430 g (4¼ cups) peeled and chopped rhubarb
- 65 g (⅓ cup) caster (superfine granulated) sugar
- 1 vanilla pod
- 2 g (1 tsp.) agar-agar powder

METHOD

1. In a saucepan combine the rhubarb, sugar, and vanilla pod and cook slowly until the mixture has reduced by almost half.
2. Add the agar-agar and whisk well.
3. Bring to a boil, continuing to whisk, then reduce the heat and simmer for 1 minute.
4. Remove the vanilla pod and then mix with a hand mixer until smooth. Let the mixture cool slightly before filling the cake.

TO FILL THE CAKE

1. Place the cake on a work surface and cover one half of the cake with cling film (plastic wrap), making sure the hole on that side is completely covered.
2. Transfer the rhubarb compote to a pastry bag fitted with a large round (1.5 cm/½ inch) tip.
3. Stand the cake upright on the cling-filmed (plastic-wrapped) side, then pipe the compote into the hole.
4. Let cool in the refrigerator for about 1 hour before serving. Once the compote is set, remove the cling film (plastic wrap) and slice the cake.

FOUR SEASONS HOTEL, TEN TRINITY SQUARE

Rotunda Lounge

*T*here are many magnificent buildings with interesting histories in the capital where you can enjoy afternoon tea, and Ten Trinity Square, positioned just a stone's throw from the Tower of London, is certainly amongst one of the best. Your first sight of the grand neo-classical building, which was erected in 1924 by the Port of London Authority, will fairly take your breath away, and the remodeled interior, which reflects its maritime history, does not disappoint. The grand entrance hall, resplendent with vast arrangements of fresh flowers, leads on to the Rotunda Lounge, where tea is served. The centrepiece of the room is undoubtedly the spectacular domed ceiling, which is a replica of the original that came crashing down during the Blitz. Plaster relief work on the walls, each section with its own wreath and crest, pays tribute to trading partners from Canada to India, whilst further engravings are a testament to commercial, navigational, and transport links.

ADDRESS: 10 Trinity Square, Clerkenwell, London EC3N 4AJ

TEL: +44 (0)20 3297 9200

WEB: www.fourseasons.com /tentrinity

AFTERNOON TEA SERVED: Friday to Sunday 3.00pm–5.30pm. A selection of afternoon tea cakes and tarts are available every other day.

SET TEAS: Ten Trinity Heritage, with or without champagne; The Royal includes a glass of Heidsieck 1995 Brut champagne

NEAREST UNDERGROUND STATIONS: Tower Hill

PLACES OF INTEREST NEARBY: Tower of London, Tower Bridge, St Katharine's Docks, Trinity Hill Memorial, HMS Belfast

As you settle down to enjoy your afternoon tea, take a minute to look at the design on the tea service, which has also been inspired by the building's previous seafaring connections. From the nautical compass in the centre of the plates, to the map of the world on the underside, the trade route taken by tea clippers between China in the East and London in the West is celebrated in style. Delicious traditional fare is the order of the day, with the Heritage tea including sandwiches, scones served with Devonshire clotted cream and seasonal jams, and dainty French pastries, along with a pot of fine leaf tea. The Royal Afternoon Tea goes a step further, including a glass of Heidsieck champagne and concluding with a slice of the daily baked cake. It's all helpful to fortify you for some serious sightseeing!

THE GORING

$\mathcal{A}$ mere stone's throw from Buckingham Palace and tucked away from the bustle of Victoria, The Goring is a rare treasure, for the hotel has been owned by the same family since it opened in 1910. It retains the feeling of an elegant, albeit large, private house, and every aspect of afternoon tea is intended to make it a relaxing occasion. So switch off your mobile, leave your laptop with the concierge, and settle down in the cosy lounge or bar, or the dining room on a Saturday, to enjoy a feast fit for royalty in tranquil, genteel surroundings.

Choose your tea from a very select list of leaf teas, including amongst the black teas the Goring's own Afternoon Blend and the Fortnum & Mason Royal Blend, first blended for King Edward VII in 1903; there are also white, oolong, and green teas as well as aromatic infusions. To begin the proceedings, you'll be served a savoury

ADDRESS: 15 Beeston Place, Westminster, London SW1W 0JW

TEL: +44 (0)20 7396 9000

EMAIL: afternoontea@thegoring.com

WEB: www.thegoring.com

AFTERNOON TEA SERVED: bar and lounge, daily sittings at 3.00pm, 3.30pm, 4.00pm; bar, lounge, and dining room, Saturday 1.00pm–4.00pm

SET TEAS: traditional, The Bollinger Tea. Gluten free can be requested in advance.

NEAREST UNDERGROUND STATIONS: Victoria

PLACES OF INTEREST NEARBY: Buckingham Palace, The Royal Mews, The Changing of the Guard, The Queen's Gallery, Knightsbridge, Mayfair, St James's Park, Green Park, Hyde Park, Kensington Palace

starter, which could, for example, be a pea puree in a glass, but this changes seasonally. The tiered cake stand that follows has finger sandwiches with some unusual fillings as well as scrumptious scones, fruit and plain, served with clotted cream and jam. The staff are always on hand to replenish your cup, refresh your pot of tea, and bring more of whatever takes your fancy. The penultimate course, described as 'cakes, bakes, fancies, and tarts' is a treat, with dainty cakes varied according to the season. If you happen to be visiting on a sunny summer afternoon, there is nowhere better to enjoy a truly traditional tea than seated at a table on the veranda or on the lawn, sipping champagne and enjoying the splendours of an English garden. But don't forget to ask for a table in one of these coveted spots when you book, and hope they can accommodate your request! In 2013, The Goring had the supreme accolade of being given the appointment of a Royal Warrant, the only hotel to have been awarded the honour for hospitality services, so you can expect nothing but the best from your afternoon tea experience.

Mince Pies

Recipe courtesy of Shay Cooper at The Goring

INGREDIENTS

Sweet Pastry

- 500 g (4 cups) plain (all-purpose) flour
- 250 g (1 cup + 1 Tbsp.) caster (superfine granulated) sugar
- 250 g (1 cup + 1 Tbsp.) butter, cubed
- 2 large eggs

Financier Batter

- 225 g (1 cup) caster (superfine granulated) sugar
- 90 g (¾ cup) ground almonds
- 180 g (1½ cups) plain (all-purpose) flour
- 7 egg whites (280 g/1 cup), lightly beaten
- 225 g (1 cup) butter

Shay Cooper updates the traditional mince pie recipe with a financier batter top, giving the pies an irresistible crunch. Keep these little pies in an airtight container for those moments when friends pay an unexpected visit. Depending on the size you make the pies, this recipe will make about 20 larger pies or 50 petit four size pies.

This recipe presents terms and measurements for both UK and US readers. Units are given first for UK readers in the original measurement units, then for US readers in converted units in parentheses. Do not mix the units. US equivalent terms are also given in parentheses where needed.

INGREDIENTS

Filling

- Dash of brandy
- Handful of chopped almonds
- 2 jars (750 g/26 oz.) organic mincemeat

To Serve

- Crème fraîche

METHOD

For baking: You'll need several shallow 12 hole bun tins (pans) or individual mini tart tins (pans).

1. Preheat the oven to 180°C (350°F).
2. To make the pastry, combine the flour and sugar in a large bowl. Rub the butter in until it resembles fine bread crumbs. Add the eggs and mix with a palette knife. Using your hands, bring the dough together. Shape into a disc, and wrap in cling film (plastic wrap). Leave to chill in the fridge for 15 to 20 minutes.
3. To make the batter, place the sugar, almonds, and flour in a food processor. Using the whisk attachment, mix on slow speed, gradually adding the egg whites, then put to one side.
4. In a saucepan melt the butter over medium heat. When it begins to change colour to a shade of hazelnut brown, pass it through a clean piece of linen or tea towel to remove any impurities.
5. While the butter is still warm, add it to the batter very gradually until it is completely incorporated and then place the batter in the refrigerator.
6. Roll out the pastry to a thickness of about 3 mm (⅛ inch). Use a fluted cutter to cut out circles slightly larger than the bun hole in your tin (pan), according to the size of the pies you are making. Reroll leftover dough and cut out again. Put the discs into floured tart tins (pans) or bun tins (pans), and bake in the oven for around ten minutes (five minutes if you are making petit four size pies), or until just crisp and lightly coloured. Take the tart pans out of the oven and place them on a wire rack to cool.
7. To make the filling, combine the brandy and nuts with the mincemeat, then spoon about 2.5 g (½ tsp.) of this mixture onto each pastry disc.
8. Add a layer of the financier batter to each pastry disc, taking care not to overfill. Smooth over with a palette knife.
9. Bake the tarts in the oven for an additional 12 minutes until the financier topping is cooked through and turns a golden brown. Cool slightly, transfer to a wire rack, and cool completely.
10. Serve topped with a spoonful of crème fraîche.

GROSVENOR HOUSE
Park Room

*I*t's very fitting to have an afternoon tea named in honour of Anna, the 7th Duchess of Bedford, for it was she who reputedly complained of having 'a sinking feeling' mid-afternoon, and who recovered her equilibrium by being served a small, light meal of sandwiches or cakes along with a dish of tea. Having set a precedent, the ritual has become a tradition and is celebrated in style in the elegant and exceedingly comfortable Park Room at Grosvenor House. The service is impeccable, the room is splendid, a pianist plays every afternoon, and you can take in the view across Park Lane to Hyde Park.

ADDRESS: 86–90 Park Lane, Mayfair, London W1K 7TN

TEL: +44 (0)20 7399 8452

EMAIL: park.room@marriott.com

WEB: www.parkroom.co.uk

AFTERNOON TEA SERVED: daily 12.30pm–6.00pm

SET TEAS: Seasonally changing traditional tea with champagne options, Grover's Children's Tea. Dietary requirements can be accommodated for with advance notice.

NEAREST UNDERGROUND STATIONS: Marble Arch, Hyde Park Corner

PLACES OF INTEREST NEARBY: Apsley House, Buckingham Palace, Hyde Park, Bond Street

The menu both follows and breaks with tradition, offering delicate closed as well as open sandwiches, with a wide range of delicious fillings and toppings. Your plate will be refreshed as often as you like before you tuck into the buttermilk scones, both plain and raisin, with clotted cream and jam. Maybe you prefer to put the clotted cream on first, following the Devonshire tradition, but regardless, there is an excellent collection of first-rate jams. The selection of British preserves are likely to include delicate rose petal, gooseberry, strawberry, raspberry, blackcurrant, and rhubarb and ginger, so you are really spoilt for choice. An assortment of home-baked cakes and tantalising afternoon tea pastries – which could include a cherry and pistachio macaron and a jasmine tea shortbread with peach compote – are divine, and change according to the season. The tea list from Newby is extensive, and the expert team will advise on how long your chosen tea leaves should brew before pouring. It's up to you to decide yourself whether to add the milk before or after, and there are no hard and fast rules, but pouring the tea first does allow you to choose the exact strength and flavour you prefer.

Children have their own special tea menu, which includes sandwiches stuffed with fillings that are bound to appeal, including banana and chocolate spread, yummy strawberry jam, and eggy mayonnaise. The treats are sure to win favour, with a miniature knickerbocker glory, a chocolate brownie, a raspberry-filled cupcake, and a healthy fresh fruit skewer with yogurt and fruit coulis. Every child goes home with their own cuddly Grover – named after the hotel's eponymous British Bulldog. Child or adult, this is an experience to remember.

HAM YARD HOTEL

*T*here is never a wrong time for tea at Ham Yard, a wonderfully quirky and stylish hotel tucked away in Ham Yard urban village, betwixt and between Regent Street, Piccadilly Circus, and Soho. Whether you are meeting friends for a break from shopping, having a pre-theatre indulgence, or celebrating a special occasion, the tea will be a treat. There are a number of spaces where you can sit, including the glass-roofed Orangery, the beautiful, comfortable Shade Bar, or in the restaurant. On a summer's day you could take tea outside on the terrace, shaded by parasols and trees and in view of Tony Cragg's impressive bronze sculpture centrepiece. The generous and affordable set tea changes weekly, and you'll enjoy savoury treats and sandwiches, the best of scones with jam and clotted cream, and delectable pastries and cakes, all served on the most beautiful Wedgwood bone china designed by

ADDRESS: 1 Ham Yard, Soho, London W1D 7DT

TEL: +44 (0)20 3642 1007

EMAIL: restaurant@hamyardhotel.com

WEB: www.firmdalehotels.com /hotels/london/ham-yard-hotel

AFTERNOON TEA SERVED: daily 12.00pm–5.00pm for the public, all day for hotel guests

SET TEAS: Traditional and Healthy Options afternoon teas. Reduced sugar, gluten-free, and vegan afternoon tea options available on request, please book in advance. Check the website for seasonal specials.

NEAREST UNDERGROUND STATIONS: Piccadilly Circus

PLACES OF INTEREST NEARBY: Theatreland, Soho, Regent Street shopping, Trafalgar Square, Piccadilly

Kit Kemp and decorated with her stunning Mythical Creatures. If you want something more substantial, for a small supplement there are savoury afternoon additions available, including the tasty Ham Yard rarebit with baby watercress. Most dietary requirements can be accommodated, preferably with advance notice. The head chef and head pastry chef are always coming up with new ideas for the cakes, macarons, desserts, scones, and jams, so the menu constantly changes. A choice of three teas is included in the price, but for a small supplement you can choose from the list of special teas and infusions. Before you head off home, wander around Ham Yard village and enjoy the mix of eclectic boutique shops.

HOTEL CAFÉ ROYAL
Oscar Wilde Bar

*Y*ou would be hard pressed to find a more opulent location in London in which to enjoy afternoon tea, for the fabulously restored, gilded, and mirrored Oscar Wilde Bar within the Hotel Café Royal is the height of decadence and the jewel in the hotel's crown. Formerly the Grill Room, which was established in 1865, this is where Oscar Wilde met and fell in love with Lord Alfred 'Bosie' Douglas, with such disastrous consequences. Aubrey Beardsley and James McNeill Whistler, members, with Wilde, of the Aesthetic art movement, met here to discuss and debate the merits of their craft, in the company of other notable but long-forgotten artists, writers, composers, and performers. A century later, Mick Jagger, the Beatles, and Elizabeth Taylor danced the night away in this very room.

ADDRESS: 68 Regent Street, Piccadilly, London W1B 4DY

TEL: +44 (0)20 7406 3310

EMAIL: restaurants@hotelcaferoyal.com

WEB: www.hotelcaferoyal.com /afternoontea

OFFERS: see www.afternoontea .co.uk/uk/london

AFTERNOON TEA SERVED: Monday to Wednesday 2.00pm, 3.00pm, 4.00pm, 5.00pm. Thursday to Sunday and bank holidays 12.00pm, 1.00pm, 2.00pm, 3.00pm, 4.00pm, 5.00pm. Advance booking highly recommended.

SET TEAS: traditional. Check website for special seasonal teas.

DRESS CODE: gentlemen are requested to wear a jacket; a tie is optional

NEAREST UNDERGROUND STATIONS: Piccadilly Circus

PLACES OF INTEREST NEARBY: Theatreland, Soho, Regent Street shopping, Trafalgar Square, Piccadilly, Trocadero Entertainment Centre

Secreted away in these surroundings, it is easy to forget the bustle of Regent Street as you settle down in the comfortable leather chairs and enjoy the feast that awaits you. Tea here is a real treat, from the amuse-bouche to the final mouthful of pastry or cake, with everything imaginable in between. There are savoury toppings on a variety of breads – do ask if you want all vegetarian – and first-rate raisin and plain scones with a golden glaze, served with clotted cream and jam (of course). The dainty delicacies which follow are just the right size, neither too small nor too big, and vary from season to season. In the unlikely event that you have any room left, for a small supplement you can enjoy a slice of one of the traditional loaf cakes displayed on the bar. An excellent tea list of over twenty blends and an optional choice of champagne are all enjoyed to the accompaniment of the resident pianist, who will happily play your request.

HOTEL DU VIN, CAMBRIDGE

*C*ambridge is awash with historic buildings, and the Hotel du Vin on Trumpington Street sits well amongst these. Not as old as many of the Grade II listed places which surround it, it nevertheless has a quiet grandeur, a reminder perhaps of its past days as a university building. King's College is at the north end of Trumpington Street, the Fitzwilliam Museum is almost opposite, and the university botanic gardens are a mere stroll down the road. So there is plenty of opportunity for sightseeing before or after your afternoon tea, which can take place in any of the comfortable spaces in the hotel. You could choose the library, the open bistro dining area where a seat by the window will give you a view of passers-by, the vaulted bar downstairs, or the small outside terrace if the weather is fine and there is room.

ADDRESS: 15–19 Trumpington Street, Cambridge, Cambridgeshire CB2 1QA

TEL: +44 (0)1223 928 991

WEB: www.hotelduvin.com /cambridge

AFTERNOON TEA SERVED: daily 12.00pm–6.00pm. Booking in advance.

SET TEAS: cream tea, traditional tea. Vegetarian and gluten-free options available, pre-order.

NEAREST MAINLINE STATIONS: Cambridge

PLACES OF INTEREST NEARBY: Fitzwilliam Museum, Museum of Archaeology and Anthropology, Museum of Zoology, Museum of Classical Archaeology, Whipple Museum of the History of Science, The Sedgwick Museum of Earth Sciences, The Polar Museum, Centre for Computing History, Kettle's Yard, punting tours on The Cam, University colleges

Afternoon tea is served alongside all-day dining and should be booked in advance. The generous and well-priced set tea reflects the French ambience of the hotel, and begins with a colourful presentation of five different savoury items, which make a nice change from traditional sandwiches. These typically include a mini quiche, an egg-filled brioche, a miniature croissant filled with ham and cheese, an open smoked salmon and cream cheese on rye, and a delicious cherry tomato, basil, and tapenade galette. Drink a tea from the tea gurus Twinings list, including The Full English and The Mighty Assam, and change the variety if you wish. Maybe enjoy a glass of Prosecco before you move on to the vintage cake stand and tackle the scones served with a selection of Bonne Maman jams and thick clotted cream. Leave room for the shot glass of refreshing gin and tonic sundae, the miniature cakes, and the cake stand's crowning glory, a stick of sweet,

fruit-flavoured, frothy candy floss. It's easy to forget the time passing by and the pull of Cambridge's innumerable attractions as you relax and enjoy tea here. And it won't stretch your purse strings too much, so you could make it a regular indulgence.

HOTEL DU VIN, HENLEY-ON-THAMES

You'll find this member of the Hotel du Vin 'family' in the delightful 12th-century market town of Henley-on-Thames, nestling at the foot of the Chilterns, and there is nowhere better in town to enjoy a jolly good, generous afternoon tea. The position is wonderful, for it is just fifty yards from the town's famous river, home to the annual five-day rowing spectacular that is the Henley Royal Regatta. The hotel sits behind a Georgian façade, within a cluster of listed buildings that were, for 300 years, home to Brakspears Brewery. Inside, you still get the feel of the history of the building, for many of the original features, including cast iron fixings, beams, columns, and brickwork, have been preserved, but there is an added contemporary sparkle and a tranquillity that makes it a lovely place to visit. Weather

ADDRESS: New Street, Henley-on-Thames, Berkshire RG9 2BP

TEL: +44 (0)1491 877 579

EMAIL: reception.henley@hotelduvin.com

WEB: www.hotelduvin.com/henley-on-thames

AFTERNOON TEA SERVED: daily 12.00pm–6.00pm

SET TEAS: cream tea, traditional tea. Gin, Prosecco, and champagne additions available. Vegan, vegetarian, and gluten-free options available.

NEAREST MAINLINE STATIONS: Henley-on-Thames

PLACES OF INTEREST NEARBY: Henley Royal Regatta, River and Rowing Museum, Stonor Park, Nuffield Place, Greys Court (National Trust)

permitting, the central courtyard is the perfect spot for a leisurely tea al fresco; otherwise the elegant and relaxed interior is just the ticket.

In a twist on the traditional, finger sandwiches are replaced with items such as a mini smoked salmon bagel, a bite-sized quiche, a galette topped with heritage tomato and tapenade, and a savoury filled croissant. You'll love the crumbly scones topped with clotted cream and strawberry jam, and that's before you get to the sweet treats. The little lemon meringue pie and the sugary doughnuts filled with rhubarb and custard never tasted so good, and there is still the gin and tonic sundae to enjoy.

Gin is a very good accompaniment to afternoon tea, and addicts can add a G and T from the list of carefully selected gins on offer, including Sipsmith Sloe Gin, Carounn, and Monkey 47, served with Fever Tree botanical tonics. Of course there is nothing quite like a restorative and refreshing cup of tea, and there is something to suit everyone on the list of

Twinings teas. So, whether you have been hiking in the Chilterns, are in the town for the Regatta, the Festival of Music and Arts, or the Henley Literary Festival, or are just strolling around and taking in the museums or the shops, don't miss the opportunity to take tea here, for it is one of the delights of Henley.

INTERCONTINENTAL LONDON, THE O2

$\mathscr{S}$ hiny and new, the ultra-modern InterContinental is perched on the edge of the Greenwich Peninsula, facing the O2 arena across the River Thames. The area is steeped in history, for the East India Company operated from near here, plying their increasingly successful trade in silk, porcelain, and especially tea. Tea owed its growing popularity as a fashionable drink to Catherine of Braganza, the Portuguese wife of King Charles II, and the company placed their first order for tea – 100 lbs (45kg) of China tea to be imported from Java to Britain – in 1664. Paying homage to the hotel's position, the Meridian Lounge, where tea is served, takes its name from the

ADDRESS: 1 Waterview Drive, Greenwich Peninsula, London SE10 0TW

TEL: +44 (0)20 8463 6868

EMAIL: meridianlounge@iclondon-theo2.com

WEB: www.iclondon-theo2.com

AFTERNOON TEA SERVED: daily 1.00pm–5.00pm (last seating 4.30pm)

SET TEAS: traditional, champagne, themed teas including Wimbledon, Easter, Mother's Day (please check the website). Special dietary requirements can be accommodated upon request. Bespoke afternoon tea master classes in partnership with East India Tea Company can be arranged upon request.

NEAREST UNDERGROUND STATIONS: North Greenwich. Also available: river transport at Thames Clipper.

PLACES OF INTEREST NEARBY: The O2 arena (there is direct access from the hotel between 9.00am and 1.00am), Canary Wharf, Royal Observatory, Royal Museums Greenwich, Cutty Sark, Riverboat service, Emirates Airline Cable Car, ExCel, Eltham Palace

meridian line in nearby Greenwich, the spot that marks the dividing point between the eastern and western hemispheres. The lounge, just off the hotel lobby, is an excellent place to enjoy the views, and on a fine day you can take advantage of the riverside terrace and enjoy your afternoon tea out of doors. Apart from the special themed teas that are offered during the year, the regular afternoon tea menu here is a twist on the traditional, with sandwiches served on a variety of breads (carrot, beetroot, and basil are favourites), scones with Madagascan vanilla, chai, sunflower, and cranberry, and a delightful selection of pretty pastries and cakes. The East India Tea Company continues to supply tea to the hotel today, and from time to time there is live music, as well as East India Tea bespoke cocktails to complement the already delightful afternoon tea.

INTERCONTINENTAL LONDON, PARK LANE
Wellington Lounge

The combination of comfort and understated elegance is striking in the light and bright Wellington Lounge, overlooking the iconic Wellington Arch at Hyde Park Corner. The hotel, which stands on the site of Her Majesty the Queen's childhood home, was opened by His Grace the 8th Duke of Wellington in 1975, and the distinguished royal heritage is reflected in the menus. If you choose the Royal tea, the savoury sandwiches include both closed and open varieties on excellent breads. The buttermilk scones that follow are simply super – you can try the recipe yourself. The pastries all have a Queen's theme, from the tipsy cake disguised as a royal hat to the coffee and walnut cake which has been reinvented as a handbag. The use of different fresh fruits reflects the changing seasons, and there is always a special Christmas

ADDRESS: 1 Hamilton Place, Park Lane, Mayfair, London W1J 7QY

TEL: +44 (0)20 7409 3131

EMAIL: wellingtonlounge@ihg.com

WEB: http://parklane.intercontinental.com

OFFERS: see www.afternoontea.co.uk/uk/london

AFTERNOON TEA SERVED: daily 1.00pm–5.00pm

SET TEAS: Royal Afternoon Tea, Vegetarian Royal Afternoon Tea, Guiltless Afternoon Tea, seasonal and festive teas. Gluten- and dairy-free options available with advance notice.

NEAREST UNDERGROUND STATIONS: Marble Arch, Hyde Park Corner, Green Park

PLACES OF INTEREST NEARBY: Hyde Park, Apsley House, Piccadilly, Buckingham Palace

afternoon tea to enjoy. The vegetarian option has an excellent selection of savoury items, whilst the Guiltless Tea is free of refined sugar and is carefully created with all-natural, nutrient-filled ingredients. The menu proves that guiltless can still be delicious, and can be tailored to any dietary requirements, including gluten and dairy free. If you need to justify adding an hour and a half of unlimited Mercier, Moët & Chandon, or Veuve Clicquot champagne to your afternoon tea, maybe think on the words of Winston Churchill: 'In success you deserve it, in defeat you need it.' Teas here are provided by the family-run Northern Tea Merchants, with a list including some exclusive blends, and there are tea ambassadors on hand to advise and tell you about any seasonal offerings. This is a thoroughly delightful lounge in which to enjoy a delicious tea.

Buttermilk Scones

Recipe courtesy of the InterContinental London, Park Lane

INGREDIENTS

- 220 g (1¾ cups) plain (all-purpose) flour
- 40 g (2 Tbsp. + 2 tsp.) caster (superfine granulated) sugar
- 18 g (1 Tbsp. + 2 tsp.) baking powder
- 40 g (2 Tbsp. + 2 tsp.) butter
- 170 g (⅔ cup) buttermilk
- 40 g (¼ cup) sultanas or golden raisins (optional)
- For egg wash: an egg yolk, lightly beaten and mixed with a drop of cold water

METHOD

1. In a large mixing bowl, mix together the flour, sugar, and baking powder. Rub in the butter until the mixture resembles fine crumbs.
2. Add the buttermilk and mix until you have a dough. Stir in the sultanas or raisins if you're using them.

What would an afternoon tea be without its scones? Try this recipe to make your own. Serve with clotted cream and strawberry jam. Makes about 8 to 10 scones.

3. Roll out the dough to 1.5 cm (½ inch) thickness, then cut out individual scones with a 5 cm (2 inch) fluted or plain edge round cutter.
4. Place on a baking tray, leaving a gap in between each one, then put the tray in the refrigerator to rest. These can be prepared earlier in the day and kept, covered loosely with some cling film (plastic wrap), for baking later on.
5. When you are ready to bake the scones, take the tray from the refrigerator and brush the top of each scone with an egg wash. Let them return to room temperature before baking them.
6. Bake at 210°C (410°F) for about 20 minutes or until golden brown.
7. Cool on a wire tray before serving warm with jam and cream.

This recipe presents terms and measurements for both UK and US readers. Units are given first for UK readers in the original measurement units, then for US readers in converted units in parentheses. Do not mix the units. US equivalent terms are also given in parentheses where needed.

THE IVY, CHELSEA GARDEN

*C*helsea is one of the chicest neighbourhoods in London, and King's Road one of its most iconic streets. It gained fame in the 1960s, and was the hub of the Swinging Sixties, the era of The Beatles, The Rolling Stones, Mary Quant, Twiggy, Vidal Sassoon, and the Mini. It's still one of London's top shopping locations, with unique boutiques, designer clothes, an interior design emporium, and antique markets, but there is also an array of cultural and historic highlights for you to enjoy. When you have finished, there is nowhere better than the Ivy, situated on the south end of King's Road, to take the weight off your feet and enjoy a lovely afternoon tea. The ambience here is divine, for the restaurant – or modern British brasserie, as it describes itself – not only has a lovely dining room,

ADDRESS: 195–197 King's Road, Chelsea, London SW3 5EQ

TEL: +44 (0)20 3301 0300

EMAIL: reservations@theivychelsea garden.com

WEB: www.theivychelseagarden.com

AFTERNOON TEA SERVED: daily 3.00pm–5.00pm

SET TEAS: cream tea, champagne afternoon tea

NEAREST UNDERGROUND STATIONS: Sloane Square

PLACES OF INTEREST NEARBY: King's Road shopping, Saatchi Gallery, Royal Court Theatre, Cadogan Hall, Royal Hospital Chelsea, National Army Museum, Chelsea Physic Garden, Carlyle's House

but also has an Orangery, a wonderful garden terrace, and lots of eclectic art. The place is spacious and beautiful, and you'll spend time just people watching. The set afternoon tea is the same menu that is served across the Ivy group, and is very good traditional British fare. Savouries include three varieties of flavoursome finger sandwiches, jolly good fruit scones with Cornish clotted cream and strawberry preserve, and a selection of cakes and small desserts. The Ivy rings the changes occasionally, so you might find you have fruit cake with cheese, a macaron, and a filled choux bun, but whatever you are served will be most enjoyable and will not cost you the earth. Champagne and a nice cup of tea are the final touch. You can request a table in the conservatory, although you can't book for the terrace; tables there are allocated on a first come, first served basis, but it's worth asking when you arrive, and most certainly worth having a stroll outside on a nice day.

THE IVY CAFÉ,
ST JOHN'S WOOD

*T*his is an excellent spot en route to or from a pilgrimage to Abbey Road, home to the famous recording studios, and a walk across the pedestrian crossing trodden by The Beatles on 8 August 1969. It's also a stone's throw from Lord's, the world-famous home of cricket. The Ivy Café – a café-style brasserie – has something to offer everyone, and although it serves food from breakfast through dinner, the afternoon tea is a terrific value. This is British comfort food at its best, enjoyed in gorgeous art deco surroundings with marble floor tiles and zingy burnt-orange leather banquettes which, along with the street tables, make it feel a bit Parisian. Note the distinctive Ivy monogrammed table napkins as you tuck in to your tea. Savouries might include a brioche roll with truffled chicken, a finger sandwich with marinated cucumber and dill, and an open smoked salmon with cream cheese and chives on rye bread. An excellent warm scone with Cornish clotted cream, strawberry preserve, and, a very nice touch,

ADDRESS: 120 St John's Wood High Street, St John's Wood, London NW8 7SG

TEL: +44 (0)20 3096 9444

EMAIL: reservations@theivycafest johnswood.com

WEB: www.theivycafestjohnswood .com

AFTERNOON TEA SERVED: Monday to Sunday 3.00pm–5.00pm

SET TEAS: cream tea, champagne afternoon tea

NEAREST UNDERGROUND STATIONS: St John's Wood

PLACES OF INTEREST NEARBY: Lord's Cricket Ground and Museum, Abbey Road Recording Studios, Regent's Park, ZSL London Zoo, Hampstead Theatre, Regent's Park canal, St John's Wood High Street shopping

some fresh berries, can be enjoyed before or after the sweet treats. And who can resist the likes of a doughnut filled with crème brûlée, an individual raspberry cheesecake, or lemon meringue pie, to say nothing of the chocolate and salted caramel mousse? The Ivy rings the changes from time to time, so check the menu online to see what's on offer when you visit. You could add champagne, or simply choose the cream tea of scones, clotted cream, and jam; with either option you have a small selection of teas, infusions, or coffee to choose from. Do ask to have your pot refreshed. This is a stylish yet casual spot, often buzzing with locals and visitors, so it can be a bit noisy, but, if you are lucky, you may catch a celebrity in here.

KENSINGTON PALACE

The Orangery

The magnificent 18th-century Orangery, situated within the tranquil gardens of Kensington Palace, is a beautiful, historic venue for tea, especially in the spring and summer months. It was built for Queen Anne as an elaborate greenhouse to protect her citrus trees from the cold winters, but she soon recognised that the building was perfect for entertaining. Sophisticated court entertainment once took place here, and although today's visitors can enjoy breakfast and lunch as well as afternoon tea in the white-scrollwork splendour of the pavilion, it is the afternoon tea that is the highlight of the Orangery's repertoire, not least of all because it is the only Royal Palace to offer it. The Orangery keeps things elegantly simple with two options for afternoon tea. The English Orangery Afternoon Tea includes an assortment of tea sandwiches with five traditional fillings, orange-scented and currant

ADDRESS: Kensington Palace, Kensington Gardens, Kensington, London W8 4PX

TEL: +44 (0)20 3166 6113

WEB: www.orangerykensington palace.co.uk/afternoon-tea

AFTERNOON TEA SERVED: daily 12.00pm–6.00pm

SET TEAS: English Orangery Afternoon Tea, Royal Afternoon Tea, children's tea. Vegetarian and gluten-free options available on request.

NEAREST UNDERGROUND STATIONS: Queensway, Gloucester Road, High Street Kensington

PLACES OF INTEREST NEARBY: Kensington Palace, Serpentine Gallery, Princess Diana Memorial Playground, Kensington Gardens

Whilst the Orangery is being renovated, afternoon tea will continue being served in a temporary Pavilion on the lawn, overlooking the Palace.

scones served with Cornish clotted cream and English strawberry jam, and dainty pastries. No seconds here, but you won't leave hungry. Royalty features in the tea list with Royal London Blend, Palace Breakfast, Afternoon at the Palace Earl Grey, and more. The Royal Afternoon Tea features the same fine fare, but with the addition of a glass of Laurent-Perrier champagne, a glass of Pimms, or mulled wine, or you could choose a glass of Merlot Rosé Spumante. The staff serve tea in a dignified and proper manner, as you'd expect in a royal venue, but are very friendly and helpful. With wonderful views over the gardens and a generous terrace for fine weather, the Orangery is a delightful place to pass a pleasant couple of hours, with or without a visit to the palace.

THE LANESBOROUGH

Céleste

$\mathcal{E}$verything is quietly understated luxury at The Lanesborough, from the welcome you receive on entering the hotel to the experience that awaits you taking tea in Céleste, the beautiful glass-roofed restaurant. Afternoon tea service starts as lunch service ends, so Céleste is almost entirely devoted to tea guests. The tables are set with crisp linen and fine bone china, gentle piano music adds to the relaxing atmosphere, and the staff are most attentive and courteous. The set afternoon tea menu changes every two months, but you can be sure that the sandwiches will be served on a variety of artisan breads, such as walnut, granary, and basil, and have appetizing fillings, perhaps egg mayonnaise and cress, coronation chicken, smoked salmon with cream cheese, or cucumber with mint. The top-notch scones, plain and raisin, are served with Devonshire clotted cream and fruit preserves, and don't miss the opportunity to

ADDRESS: 1 Lanesborough Place, Hyde Park Corner, Belgravia, London SW1X 7TA

TEL: +44 (0)20 7259 5599

EMAIL: afternoontea@lanesborough.com

WEB: www.lanesborough.com

AFTERNOON TEA SERVED: Céleste, Monday to Friday 2.30pm–4.30pm, Saturday and Sunday 3.00pm–4.30pm. The Withdrawing Room, daily 1.00pm–5.30pm.

SET TEAS: traditional, champagne, children's on Saturdays and Sundays, festive teas including Easter, Mother's Day, and Christmas. Gluten, vegetarian, and dairy-free options are also available when booked in advance.

NEAREST UNDERGROUND STATIONS: Hyde Park Corner

PLACES OF INTEREST NEARBY: Hyde Park, Knightsbridge, Admiralty Arch, Apsley House

try some of the wonderful homemade lemon curd for a change and a real burst of flavour. The pastries reflect whatever is the current theme, and might have a Parisian twist, but all will have been intricately prepared and hand

crafted by the talented pastry chefs. On the weekends, there is a special children's tea, and it could be hard for the adults to resist the waffles served with Nutella or a choice of ice cream, or keep their hands off the hot chocolate with marshmallows.

Drinking tea here is exceptionally worthwhile, for The Lanesborough was the first London hotel to engage a Tea Sommelier, who is there to advise you on your choice of leaf to accompany the various courses. The connoisseur afternoon tea menu is extensive and includes white teas, Rooibos teas, oolong teas, six green teas, and whole leaf herbal teas. The three premium teas are Jasmine Pearls, the truly magnificent Formosa Oolong Top Fancy (also known as Asian beauty), and China Kekecha, a yellow tea which is becoming increasingly rare. The Darjeeling First Flush Goomtee is yet another star on the list, one of those sometimes referred to as the 'champagne' of Indian tea. Amongst the black teas are Bohea Lapsang Souchong, Darjeeling Jungpana, and three Lanesborough Signature blends, with an Afternoon Tea that is a lively and refreshing bespoke blend of black and green leaves with a golden cup and enticing floral aroma. Only leaf tea is served here, but you won't catch sight of a strainer, for this is ingeniously fitted inside the silver teapot, saving you any effort at all.

As an alternative to Céleste, you might prefer to take tea in the light, elegant setting of the Withdrawing Room, a sumptuously decorated room with hand-painted trompe l'oeil marbling, chandeliers, and comfortable armchairs and sofas where tea is served from 1.00pm. The atmosphere here is quite different, but the afternoon tea is the same delicious fare. If, by any chance, there are any pastries left, you are more than welcome to take them home in a neat box to enjoy later.

Rocher Praline

Recipe courtesy The Lanesborough

Hazelnut Streusel

INGREDIENTS

- 500 g (2¼ cups) butter
- 500 g (2¼ cups) caster (superfine granulated) sugar
- 500 g (4 cups + 3 Tbsp.) T 55 (strong white flour) (or bread flour)
- 450 g (4 cups) hazelnut powder
- 10 g (2 tsp.) salt

METHOD

1. In a large bowl, mix the butter and sugar together. Add the flour, hazelnut powder, and salt, and combine.
2. Roll the dough to approximately 2 mm (1⁄16 inch) thickness, then cut into discs of 30 mm (1⅛ inches) in diameter.

Milk Chocolate Mousse

INGREDIENTS

- 90 g (¼ cup + 2 Tbsp.) double cream (heavy cream)

*F*ollow the diagram to assemble this many-layered and many-flavoured dessert.

This recipe presents terms and measurements for both UK and US readers. Units are given first for UK readers in the original measurement units, then for US readers in converted units in parentheses. Do not mix the units. US equivalent terms are also given in parentheses where needed.

- 135 g (½ cup + 1 Tbsp.) whole milk
- 4 egg yolks (90 g/⅓ cup)
- 185 g (6½ oz.) Valrhona Jivara chocolate (broken/chopped)
- 3 gelatin leaves
- 200 g (1¾ cups) double cream (heavy cream) (whipped to stiff peaks)

METHOD

1. In a heavy saucepan, combine the milk, cream (90 g/¼ cup + 2 Tbsp.), yolks, and chocolate and cook over low heat, stirring constantly, until it registers 90°C (194°F) on a cooking thermometer. Then add the gelatin, stirring well. Let the mixture cool.
2. Quickly fold in all of the 200 g (1¾ cups) of whipped cream.

Praline Insert

INGREDIENTS

- 200 g (¾ cup + 1 Tbsp.) double cream (heavy cream)
- 2 gelatin leaves
- 100 g (¾ cup) sugared almonds and hazelnuts (almond and hazelnut praline à l'ancienne)

METHOD

1. In a heavy saucepan, warm half of the cream and then add the gelatin. Add the sugared almonds and hazelnuts, then slowly add the rest of the cream. Mix.

Milk Chocolate Glaze

INGREDIENTS

- 900 g (32 oz) Valrhona Jivara chocolate
- 150 g (⅔ cup) vegetable oil
- 300 g (2 cups) hazelnuts, chopped and roasted

METHOD

1. In a heavy saucepan, combine the chocolate and oil and melt over low heat, stirring constantly. Then add the nuts and mix.

Chantilly Praline

INGREDIENTS

- 50 g (¼ cup) hazelnut praline 60%
- 20 g (2 tsp.) mascarpone cheese
- 200 g (¾ cup + 1 Tbsp.) double cream (heavy cream)

METHOD

1. In a large mixing bowl, combine the praline and mascarpone, then add the cream. Beat until you have a whipped to stiff peaks consistency.

Assembly

1. Assemble the rocher praline following the diagram. If possible, use a commercial mould.

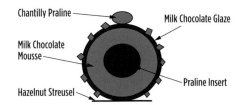

Chantilly Praline
Milk Chocolate Glaze
Milk Chocolate Mousse
Praline Insert
Hazelnut Streusel

THE LANGHAM
The Palm Court

The Langham has been beguiling guests since it first opened in 1865, and although the hotel is now firmly placed in the 21st century, the magnificent Palm Court has lost none of its original style and glamour. Famed as the place where the tradition of afternoon tea was born more than 150 years ago, the room cannot fail to dazzle. As you walk through the jewelled gates into a room resplendent with silvered ceiling, art deco glass, and gold-encrusted walls, you know you are in a special place. The tables are set with beautiful 'Langham Rose' Wedgwood china, crisp linen, and fresh flowers, all a reflection of the care and attention to detail which makes this a special place. The Langham's bespoke afternoon tea

ADDRESS: 1c Portland Place, Regent Street, Marylebone, London W1B 1JA

TEL: +44 (0)20 7636 1000

EMAIL: book@palm-court.co.uk

WEB: www.palm-court.co.uk

OFFERS: see www.afternoontea .co.uk/uk/london

AFTERNOON TEA SERVED: daily 12.15pm–5.30pm

SET TEAS: Wedgwood Afternoon Tea, High Tea with Wedgwood, with various champagne offers

NEAREST UNDERGROUND STATIONS: Oxford Circus

PLACES OF INTEREST NEARBY: Oxford Street, Regent Street, Regent's Park, British Broadcasting Corporation

begins with an amuse-bouche before you settle back and enjoy the selection of sandwiches, which are a definite cut above the ordinary and replenished as often as you like. The scones from the Palm Court bakery are warm and fluffy, and the selection of pastries and cakes, created by executive pastry chef Andrew Gravett and his team, all evoke the

Wedgwood theme and taste as beautiful as they look. Included could be a Paris Brest, the crunchiest of choux pastry encasing a lightened pecan cream, or a dainty slice of caramelized puff pastry with vanilla-infused mascarpone and strawberry coulis.

An alternative is the high tea, with an extra savoury course from which to choose. You might try the crisp parcel of smoked salmon and brie with preserved lemon and granny smith apple, or maybe the green asparagus salad with egg mimosa and smoked duck breast. As you would expect from an afternoon tea of this calibre, the selection of teas on offer is exemplary, and the tea sommelier is on hand to advise you. The five Langham Blends have been created by Alex Probyn, Master of Tea, and include a complex blend created for the 150th anniversary of the hotel, as well as a blend for children. He is also responsible for the Wedgwood Tea Collection, with teas selected with integrity and care and harvested at precisely the right moment to capture the unique natural aromas and flavours of each individual tea garden. This is a truly wonderful venue for a memorable tea.

Paris Brest

Recipe courtesy The Langham

Choux Pastry

INGREDIENTS

- 25 g (1 Tbsp. + 2 tsp.) water
- 25 g (1 Tbsp. + 2 tsp.) milk
- Pinch of caster (superfine granulated) sugar
- Pinch of salt
- 22 g (1 Tbsp. + 2 tsp.) butter
- 27 g (¼ cup) plain (all-purpose) flour
- 1 egg (50 g/¼ cup)

METHOD

1. In a heavy saucepan, combine the water, milk, sugar, salt, and butter. Bring to a rolling boil.
2. When the butter has completely melted, slowly add the flour and stir vigorously over the heat.
3. Transfer the mixture to a medium-size bowl and beat for a couple of minutes before adding the egg.

You won't be able to resist the temptation to taste as you whip up this delicious dessert.

This recipe presents terms and measurements for both UK and US readers. Units are given first for UK readers in the original measurement units, then for US readers in converted units in parentheses. Do not mix the units. US equivalent terms are also given in parentheses where needed.

Whipped Pecan Cream

INGREDIENTS

- 120 g (1 cup) water
- 22 g (3 Tbsp.) non-fat powdered milk
- 5.8 g (1½ tsp.) sugar
- 20 g (2 Tbsp.) gelatin
- 152 g (5.4 oz.) praline pecans
- 80 g (3 Tbsp.) food-grade cocoa butter, melted
- 2 egg whites (72 g/¼ cup)
- 1.2 g (¼ tsp.) salt
- 126 g (½ cup) double cream (heavy cream)

METHOD

1. In a heavy saucepan, combine the water and powdered milk. Bring the mixture to a boil and then add the gelatin. Add the pecans and cocoa butter and mix thoroughly.
2. Add the egg whites, salt, and cream and, using a stick blender, blend until smooth.
3. Allow to sit overnight in the refrigerator to set.

Craquelin

INGREDIENTS

- 74 g (⅓ cup + 1 Tbsp.) light brown sugar
- 60 g (¼ cup) butter
- 74 g (½ cup + 2 Tbsp.) plain (all-purpose) flour

METHOD

1. In a medium-size bowl, mix the sugar, butter, and flour to a thick paste using a spatula.
2. Transfer the mixture onto silicone paper, cover with another sheet, and roll out to a thickness of approximately 1 to 2 mm (1/16 inch).
3. Place the layered sheets in the freezer.

FINISHING AND PRESENTATION

1. Using a pastry bag fitted with a plain 6 mm (⅛ inch) piping nozzle, pipe the choux pastry into rings of 4 cm (1½ inches) with a 1 cm (⅜ inch) hole in the middle onto parchment paper or a silicone sheet. (This may be frozen and used at a later stage.)
2. Cut out a 4 cm (1½ inch) ring of the craquelin with a 1 cm (⅜ inch) hole in the centre and place onto each choux ring.
3. Bake the choux in a 180ºC (350ºF) oven for approximately 10 to 12 minutes.
4. Place the baked rings on a wire rack to cool and then slice in half.
5. Whip the pecan cream until a pipable texture has been achieved.
6. Using a piping bag fitted with a with a 6 mm (⅛ inch) star nozzle, pipe the cream onto one half of each circle. Place the other half of the circle on top, making sure the craquelin side is showing.
7. Dust with a thin veil of icing (confectioners') sugar before serving.

MANDARIN ORIENTAL
The Rosebery Lounge

*T*he Rosebery Lounge, inside the elegant and luxurious Mandarin Oriental hotel, overlooks cosmopolitan Knightsbridge, so it is the perfect place to take a break from shopping. There has been a hotel on the site since 1889, when it opened as a private 'Gentleman's Club', and, following a devastating fire, it reopened in 1902 as London's newest and most impressive hotel. It is still very grand, attracting royalty and celebrities galore, and, if you are celebrating a really special occasion, you can request permission from the Royal Parks to enter through the original 'Royal' entrance on the Hyde Park side. Otherwise, you'll enter from Knightsbridge, be dazzled by the marble everywhere, mount the splendid entrance staircase, and be directed to the Rosebery Lounge. The salon is actually made up of two interconnected rooms, which gives each of them a cosy feel. Furnished with comfortable chairs and sofas, the contemporary and stylish décor is echoed throughout, and there are masses of fresh flowers everywhere. The tables are set with etched glassware and elegant bone china decorated with swirling floral patterns and gilding, all designed especially for the hotel. The ambience is light and airy, enhanced by the mirrored panels and colourful artwork, and, on a chilly day, there is a fire glowing in the fabulous fireplace.

The proceedings start with the presentation of a warm, fragrant, moist hand towel, and once you have cleansed your hands, you are ready to begin. There is no sign of

ADDRESS: 66 Knightsbridge, Knightsbridge, London SW1X 7LA

TEL: +44 (0)20 77201 3828

EMAIL: molon-rosebery@mohg.com

WEB: www.mandarinoriental.com /london/hyde-park/luxury-hotel

AFTERNOON TEA SERVED: daily 12.00pm–7.30pm (last sitting)

SET TEAS: traditional, champagne, Teamaster's Choice Afternoon Tea, Beer Afternoon Tea, Sake Afternoon Tea, children's tea for those under 12. Gluten-free, vegan, and vegetarian menus available on request, preferably in advance.

NEAREST UNDERGROUND STATIONS: Knightsbridge, Hyde Park Corner

PLACES OF INTEREST NEARBY: Harvey Nichols, Harrods, Hyde Park, Green Park, Sloane Street and Knightsbridge designer shopping, Natural History Museum, Science Museum, Royal Albert Hall

the familiar tiered cake stand here, but rather a quirky metal floor stand with branches that represent the trees in Hyde Park, adorned with mandarin fruit. The set tea follows tradition, more or less, with bite-sized sandwiches – no triangles or fingers here, but rather interesting shaped ones, made up of just one piece of bread, with the filling placed on top and then the bread pinched together to form a small round. In a complete reversal of running order, the Rosebery serves the picture-perfect pastries and miniature cakes next, leaving the fresh-from-the-oven, nicely browned and glazed scones until last. Besides the rich clotted cream, there is a selection of very fruity strawberry jam, lemon curd, and a delicate and quite divine rose petal jelly. The tea list here is extensive, with the rare and limited ones, including the Taiwanese Oriental Beauty and Fujian China Da Hong Pao, attracting a supplementary cost. The staff are most attentive, and try to anticipate your requirements before you had thought of the need. Teapots are regularly refilled or replaced with a different kind of leaf, fresh cups, plates, and cutlery appear as if by magic, and nothing is too much trouble. It's easy to spend a couple of hours here enjoying an elegant take on the traditional afternoon tea.

MARRIOTT HOTEL, COUNTY HALL

Library Lounge

*W*alking through the grand archway and into County Hall is like stepping back in time, for the building is steeped in history. Opened in 1922 by King George V and Queen Mary, it survived a bombing raid during the Second World War, and was subsequently the one-time home of the Greater London Council, where many infamous battles took place between politicians in the 1980s. The walls of the splendid Library Lounge are lined with oak bookcases, topped with busts of Milton, Shakespeare, Agrippa, Plato, and other classical figures, and the alcoves now offer guests

ADDRESS: London County Hall, Westminster Bridge Road, Lambeth, London SE1 7PB

TEL: +44 (0)20 7902 8055

WEB: www.marriott.co.uk/hotels /travel/lonch-london-marriott-hotel-county-hall

AFTERNOON TEA SERVED: daily 2.30pm–4.30pm. Booking recommended.

SET TEAS: traditional, champagne with a free-flowing option

NEAREST UNDERGROUND STATIONS: Westminster, Waterloo

PLACES OF INTEREST NEARBY: Houses of Parliament, Big Ben, River Thames, Westminster Abbey, South Bank and riverside walk, St James's Park, London Eye, London Aquarium, London Dungeon, Shrek's Adventure

an intimate space in which to enjoy their afternoon tea. A small party can be seated in the privacy of the ex-librarian's office, tucked away behind the carved fireplace at the south end of this majestic room. As you take in the view of the Thames and Westminster Bridge, enjoy the generous offering before you. There are delicious sandwiches on unusual bread (if you are a vegetarian, any of the meat ones can be replaced with an alternative), savoury items, and both sweet and savoury scones. Somewhat different from tradition, you'll be served sweet English Braeburn apple and cinnamon scones as well as Montgomery Cheddar and Hampshire watercress savoury ones. Following will be a dessert in a shot glass – something like a coconut panna cotta with a pineapple and lime compote – and a selection of delicate cakes and pastries. Choose from the selection of teas, add a glass of bubbly, and sit back and have a lovely afternoon.

THE MILESTONE HOTEL

The Milestone is no ordinary hotel, for it has an old world charm and calmness about it that is in marked contrast to its position on the busy Kensington High Street. From the moment that the uniformed doorman greets you at the entrance to the grand late-Victorian building, to the time that you leave, you can be sure of the most attentive service. Tea is generally served in the cosy wood-panelled Park Lounge, a room that is reminiscent of a gentleman's study in a grand English house. Here there are huge bookcases, rich fabrics, deep cushioned armchairs, settees, and an open fire glowing in the winter months. Alternatively, you might prefer the elegant surroundings of Cheneston's restaurant or the light-filled conservatory, decked out in dramatic black and white fabrics and floor tiles.

ADDRESS: 1 Kensington Court, Kensington, London W8 5DL

TEL: +44 (0)20 7917 1000

EMAIL: bookms@rchmail.com

WEB: www.milestonehotel.com

AFTERNOON TEA SERVED: daily at 1.00pm, 3.00pm, and 5.00pm. Private afternoon teas by arrangement. Also available to book are Tea Tutorials with the Tea Academy. There is a 'Picnic in the Park' service available to order.

SET TEAS: traditional, champagne, Royal, Little Prince and Princess (for children under 12), Gentlemanly (requires 24 hours' notice), seasonal teas including Halloween and Festive teas, vegetarian, gluten free

NEAREST UNDERGROUND STATIONS: High Street Kensington

PLACES OF INTEREST NEARBY: Kensington Gardens, Kensington Palace, Hyde Park, Royal Albert Hall, Serpentine Gallery

The traditional set tea is a ritual fit for royalty. It strikes the perfect balance of savoury and sweet, with finger sandwiches bursting with delicious fillings, including an unusual and delicious circular chicken mayonnaise rolled in flaked almonds, and smoked salmon served on dark walnut and raisin bread. Freshly-baked scones with Devonshire clotted cream and homemade strawberry preserve precede the mouthwatering selection of French pastries, which might include éclairs, tartlets, macarons, and a delectable mini dessert. The Gentlemanly afternoon tea offers guests the opportunity to enjoy a much more savoury first course, with treats such as kataifi-wrapped prawns, spiced duck leg croquette, and a mini beef Wellington. Besides the plain and fruit scones, there are maple-cured bacon ones served with truffle butter, followed by the choice of pastries. This tea can be served with the addition of a cocktail, a flight of selected whiskies, or, for the real connoisseur, a measure of the exquisite 1989 Dalmore Constellation. Champagne lovers can add a glass, or even a bottle, of bubbly from a very good list, and enjoy strawberries and cream to go with it. For children, the bespoke menu includes bite-sized delicacies, crustless sandwiches, mini pastries, doughnuts, and hot chocolate. The young people also have the opportunity to don chef's whites and decorate their own cupcake, and are presented with a certificate to take home.

The list of leaf teas here is first rate. Choose from a strong Ceylon breakfast tea to Planters Mistress, a light golden scented tea described as a 'scandalous take on a much cherished aristocratic classic'. There are seasonally picked Single Estate Teas from as far afield as Nuwareliya, Assam, Hatton, and Darjeeling, and don't forget the unusual and exciting teas such as Pink Tea, Silver Tips, and Chocolate Heaven. If you are of a mind, you can also book a tutorial with the Tea Academy, with either a taster tea menu or the full afternoon tea, and learn more about the glorious tradition of afternoon tea. And for the ultimate summer treat you can order a picnic in the park. Truly indulgent.

Shortbread

Recipe courtesy The Milestone Hotel

INGREDIENTS

- 340 g (2¾ cups) plain (all-purpose) flour
- 95 g (⅓ cup + 1 Tbsp.) sugar
- 3 g (½ tsp.) salt
- 250 g (1 cup + 2 Tbsp.) butter

Bea Tollman is President and Founder of the boutique Red Carnation Hotel Collection, which also includes The Summer Lodge Country House Hotel in Dorset, where this delicious shortbread is placed in every guest's room. This recipe is from her cookbook *A Life in Food*.

METHOD

1. Place the butter into the freezer for a few hours before starting to make the shortbread.
2. In a large mixing bowl, combine the flour, sugar, and salt.
3. Grate the frozen butter and mix with the dry ingredients until the mixture resembles coarse bread crumbs; don't overmix.
4. Line a 23 cm (9 inch) square tin (pan) with parchment paper. Add the flour-butter mixture, pressing down slightly to flatten the top (it should be approximately 3 cm/1 inch high).
5. Bake at 120°C (250°F) for 55 minutes.
6. After removing the tin (pan) from the oven, sprinkle the top of the shortbread with a little sugar. Let it cool completely before cutting; overnight is best.

This recipe presents terms and measurements for both UK and US readers. Units are given first for UK readers in the original measurement units, then for US readers in converted units in parentheses. Do not mix the units. US equivalent terms are also given in parentheses where needed.

MONDRIAN LONDON

Dandelyan Bar

*W*alking into Dandelyan cocktail bar, named after the bar impresario, Ryan Chetiyawardana, aka Mr Lyan, is a surprise in itself, but this is only the first of many, as you are about to experience a unique afternoon tea with a botanical twist. The 70s-inspired Wyld afternoon tea, served in the Mondrian's playful, bubble gum-hued and riverfront Dandelyan cocktail bar, combines deceptively light yet potent cocktails with an afternoon tea which veers off the traditional. Creative drinks, concocted by award-winning mixologist Mr Lyan, are paired with sweet and savoury bites, providing a seamless fusion of inviting botanical flavours. The botanical theme is echoed in the tableware, with Portmeirion's Botanic Garden pottery gracing the table.

The four courses start with delicious savoury items, and you can expect the likes of a leek and goat's cheese rarebit on 7-grain toast and a chicken pinwheel sandwich

paired with Lyan Lager braised bacon jam. Finger sandwiches have equally inventive fillings. The dessert offerings are distinctly retro, from the ever-popular Battenberg cake, a miniature custard tart dusted with nutmeg, a pine-scented baked Alaska which is sure to transport you back to the 1970s, and a shortbread which marries caraway with rose blancmange – yet another rave from the pudding grave. Each course is paired with a botanical cocktail; exclusive combinations might include the Fluff and Fold Royale with lime, fresh basil, cacao liqueur, orange bitters and Prosecco. One cocktail will be palate cleansing, like the refreshing Bankside Swizzle, made with pineapple cordial, citrus, and lemon balm. Cocktails are served alongside hand-blended loose-leaf tea from Camellia's Tea House, and the menus change, so you will be in for a surprise no matter when you go.

ADDRESS: 20 Upper Ground, Southwark, London SE1 9PD

TEL: +44 (0)20 3747 1063

EMAIL: dandelyanrsvp@mondrianlondon.com

WEB: www.morganshotelgroup .com/mondrian/mondrian-london

AFTERNOON TEA SERVED: Thursday to Sunday 12.00pm– 5.00pm (please check for extended service)

SET TEAS: Wyld Afternoon Tea (including cocktails), Boozeless and Champagne options available

NEAREST UNDERGROUND/ MAINLINE STATIONS: Waterloo, Blackfriars

PLACES OF INTEREST NEARBY: Tate Modern, River Thames, The Globe Theatre, Borough Market, National Theatre, OXO Tower

THE NED

Millie's Lounge

Millie's Lounge in The Ned has to be amongst one of the trendiest places in the capital to enjoy a traditional afternoon tea. The hotel and member's club, bang in the heart of the City of London, takes its name from the architect, Sir Edwin 'Ned' Lutyens, who designed the building back in the 1920s as the headquarters of Midland Bank, then the largest clearing bank in the world. The ground floor, all 3,000 square metres (9,800 square feet) of it, was the banking hall, and has been skillfully and sympathetically divided up by majestic Verdite columns and rows of original Grade 1 listed walnut banking counters to create a distinct space for each of the eight restaurants. The centerpiece is the former reception desk, now

ADDRESS: 27 Poultry, City of London, London EC2R 8AJ

TEL: +44 (0)20 3828 2000

EMAIL: restaurants@thened.com

WEB: www.thened.com

AFTERNOON TEA SERVED: Monday to Saturday 2.00pm–5.00pm

SET TEAS: traditional, champagne, Mini Afternoon Tea

NEAREST UNDERGROUND STATIONS: Bank

PLACES OF INTEREST NEARBY: Bank of England Museum, Monument, Mansion House, Guildhall Great Hall, Guildhall Art Gallery, City of London Police Museum, Wren's St Margaret Lothbury Church, London Wall, Leadenhall Market

transformed into a stage for daily live music performances, which can be seen from Millie's Lounge. Carpeted and cosy, with intimate seating areas, you can just sit back and make yourself comfortable whilst the friendly staff take care of you. Marble-topped tables are set with bespoke Green Hibiscus Burleighware, and the traditional British afternoon tea, which is served alongside the all-day menu, won't break the bank. If you are just peckish, then opt for scones and a cuppa; otherwise, the full tea follows tradition with finger sandwiches, fat fruit and plain scones and supporting cast of jam and clotted cream, followed by a nice selection of dainty pastries. You can be sure that there will be a slice of Battenberg cake, but the others change on a daily basis, so you can come back time and again and expect something different. The Ned is a vibrant location and in a super spot for sightseeing around the city, just the ticket for a break during the afternoon.

NUMBER SIXTEEN

The Orangery

*O*nce you cross the threshold of Number Sixteen, you'll find it hard to believe that you are a mere stone's throw from the hustle and bustle of South Kensington, with its collection of world-class museums, fabulous concert hall, and grand park. Number Sixteen forms part of a mid-Victorian terrace resplendent with a distinctive white stucco exterior and grand portico, but the interior of this boutique hotel is a million miles away from its historic heritage. Eclectic and surprising, you can expect to spend a relaxing time here enjoying afternoon tea, which is served in The Orangery or, weather permitting, in the private garden. Do bear in mind that you can't reserve a table outside, only request one, but even if you are not seated outside, you can still take a stroll around this secret haven where coy carp swim lazily in the pond and lush greenery and sun umbrellas provide shade.

ADDRESS: 16 Sumner Place, Kensington, London SW7 3EG

TEL: +44 (0)20 7589 5232

EMAIL: sixteen@firmdale.com

WEB: www.firmdalehotels.com /hotels/london/number-sixteen /location

AFTERNOON TEA SERVED: daily 12.00pm–5.30pm

SET TEAS: gluten free, vegetarian, and vegan options available on request. For occasional celebratory teas, see the website. Rosé Champagne and Bellini options available.

NEAREST UNDERGROUND STATIONS: South Kensington

LOCAL INTEREST: Royal Albert Hall, Hyde Park, Victoria and Albert Museum, The Albert Memorial, Science Museum, Natural History Museum, The Brompton (London) Oratory, Kensington Gardens

Tables are laid with crisp white linen runners and napkins and set with the hotel's distinctive Wedgwood bone china adorned with Kit Kemp's unique design of whimsical and lyrical Mythical Creatures. For a very reasonable cost, you'll be served a selection of traditional sandwiches and a savoury item, good scones with preserves and clotted cream, and an assortment of cakes which, as the menu changes during the year, might include carrot cake, Battenberg, a chocolate brownie, and a strawberry cupcake. The leaf tea menu included in the price is small, with a breakfast, an Earl Grey, and a second flush Darjeeling, but for a small supplement you can choose from the special teas and infusions. This is altogether a very civilized place to unwind.

OLD PARSONAGE HOTEL

$\mathscr{O}$xford's dreaming spires are within walking distance of the Old Parsonage Hotel, but the hotel is just far enough away from the hustle and bustle of the city to allow you to relax. The 17th-century building has an illustrious history, having survived the English Civil War, and as you walk through the front doorway, with its heavy oak door and original hinges and door nails, spare a moment to imagine who has crossed the threshold over the course of more than 300 years. On a warm summer's day there is nowhere better to enjoy your excellent afternoon tea than the walled front terrace, seated at weathered tables set with nice white china, silverware, fine linen table mats, and napkins. Otherwise, you will be very comfortable indeed in the Parsonage Grill. The room has an intimate atmosphere about it, and a roaring

ADDRESS: 1–3 Banbury Road, Oxford, Oxfordshire OX2 6NN

TEL: +44 (0)1865 310 210

EMAIL: restaurant@oldparsonage-hotel.co.uk

WEB: www.oldparsonage-hotel .co.uk

AFTERNOON TEA SERVED: Monday to Saturday 2.30pm–5.00pm, Sunday 3.30pm–6.00pm

SET TEAS: Very Savoury Tea, Very High Tea, Celebration Tea, Light Tea (scones and tea only). Gluten-free and vegetarian options always available; vegan option needs to be pre-ordered.

NEAREST MAINLINE STATIONS: Oxford

PLACES OF INTEREST NEARBY: Oxford colleges including All Souls and Magdalen, Ashmolean Museum, University Museum of Natural History, Pitt Rivers Museum, Museum of the History of Science, Sheldonian, Bodleian Library, Radcliffe Camera

log fire will warm you on colder days. You'll be hard-pressed not to spend some time looking at the art displayed here, for every square inch of the Russian Red walls is covered with oil paintings of illustrious Oxford academic and literary figures and the unique Oxford cartoons.

As for the tea, be prepared for a small feast of dainty, well-filled finger sandwiches, really good, light scones, and excellent strawberry jam with whole fruits in it. If you are having the Celebration Tea, you'll also get two other jams, possibly raspberry and delicious damson. Refills of sandwiches and scones are freely available, but leave some room for the little cakes. A chocolate brownie, a dainty pastry case filled with a tart apple filling and topped with squidgy meringue, an individual coffee walnut cake, and a cheese cake are typically on the top tier, with seasonal variations. The Very High Tea has savoury items, including a tasty gamey-coated Scotch egg, a gherkin-topped terrine, a Cornish pasty, and various patés

served with sourdough toast soldiers. Cheese scones complete the rather different treat. Add a nice, strong cup of tea, a glass of champagne, and what more could you ask for?

Macarons

Recipe courtesy Old Parsonage Hotel

INGREDIENTS

- 350 g (3 cups) icing (confectioners') sugar
- 250 g (2 cups) ground almonds
- 6 egg whites (240 g/¾ cup)
- 150 g (⅔ cup) caster (superfine granulated) sugar
- Your choice of food colouring and flavouring

METHOD

1. In a large bowl sift the icing (confectioners') sugar and almonds twice, and then mix to combine.
2. In a small bowl whisk the egg whites until stiff, and then slowly add the caster (superfine granulated) sugar.
3. Slowly fold the almond/sugar mixture into the egg white mixture until incorporated.
4. Add your choice of flavouring and food colouring.
5. Line two baking sheets with parchment paper, or use silicone mats.

This classic French dessert is not the easiest to execute, but well worth the effort.

6. Transfer the mixture to a pastry bag. Using a 1 cm (½ inch) nozzle, pipe individual macarons approximately 3 cm (1 inch) in diameter onto the baking sheets, leaving a 2 cm (¾ inch) gap between each. Give the baking sheets a sharp tap and let sit for 10 minutes.
7. Bake for 14 minutes at 145°C (293°F) on a low fan, preferably in a convection oven. (Without a convection oven, raise the temperature to 150°C/302°F and do not use the bottom shelf. The temperature needs to be steady and low; too high and the macarons will burn, too low and they will not cook through.) Transfer to a wire rack and cool thoroughly. Sandwich two macaron halves with a layer of buttercream filling (see below).

To make the buttercream filling: Beat two parts of sifted icing (confectioners') sugar with 1 part softened butter until smooth. Add your choice of flavouring and food colouring.

This recipe presents terms and measurements for both UK and US readers. Units are given first for UK readers in the original measurement units, then for US readers in converted units in parentheses. Do not mix the units. US equivalent terms are also given in parentheses where needed.

ONE ALDWYCH

The question here is whether author Roald Dahl would have ever imagined that his classic 1964 tale, *Charlie and the Chocolate Factory*, would be the inspiration for a 'scrumdiddlyumptious' afternoon tea. But that is exactly what has happened and is what you can expect at One Aldwych. The hotel sits at the end of The Strand, almost opposite Waterloo Bridge, and is one of the most prestigious Edwardian buildings in London. In the past, it was home to the *Morning Post* newspaper, the Ministry of Defence, and Lloyds Bank, amongst others. Afternoon tea is generally served in the Indigo restaurant, overlooking the hotel's impressive lobby bar and lounge, and from the outset you can see that your tea is going to be something a little bit different.

On the savoury side, there are delicious sandwiches, some of them open, with the likes of smoked salmon, egg mayonnaise, and

ADDRESS: 1 Aldwych, Covent Garden, London WC2B 4BZ

TEL: +44 (0)20 7300 0400

EMAIL: foodandbeverage reservations@onealdwych.com

WEB: www.onealdwych.com

AFTERNOON TEA SERVED:
Monday to Saturday
12.30pm–3.30pm,
Sunday 12.30pm–5.30pm.
Tea sittings are for two hours.

SET TEAS: traditional, children's tea. Gluten-free, vegan, and vegetarian options are available.

NEAREST UNDERGROUND STATIONS: Charing Cross, Covent Garden

PLACES OF INTEREST NEARBY: Covent Garden, Royal Opera House, Somerset House, The Courtauld Institute, London Transport Museum, The Theatre Museum, The British Museum, London Film Museum, Theatre Royal Drury Lane

coronation chicken toppings or fillings on poppy seed, onion, and a brioche bread, along with bite-sized quiches and a slice of a tasty tart. Don't be shy about asking for seconds. The sweet course in particular will remind you of *Charlie and the Chocolate Factory*, with a mini bottle of chocolate caramel milk, lemon and white chocolate cake pops, and homemade candy floss, good enough for Willy Wonka, to say nothing of the famous golden egg. Instead of a lucky ticket, the golden egg is filled with vanilla cheesecake and mandarin – no doubt something Augustus Gloop would enjoy. There are mini brioche and chocolate financiers, a fresh fruit Eton mess, and, of course, scones, with Devonshire clotted cream, jam, and apple and meadowsweet compote. Choose from a small but select list of teas, from Canton Teas, and perhaps have a delicious Cocktail Charlie or champagne as well. Come Christmas season – mid-November to New Year's Day – this wondrous and generous afternoon tea takes on a festive twist, reflecting the wit and wonder of Roald Dahl's classic tale.

OXO TOWER RESTAURANT

The views from the eighth floor of the OXO Tower, and especially the 75-metre (250-foot) terrace that runs along the riverside, are breathtaking, and offer a spectacular panorama across the north bank of London's skyline, taking in the majestic dome of St Paul's Cathedral, the mighty River Thames, and the City of London. This iconic building has been a South Bank landmark since the 1980s when it was owned by the makers of the famous Oxo brand. Externally, it retains its industrial heritage, but inside, all is contemporary décor and airy spaciousness, and the restaurant is an exceptional location for a really good, generous afternoon tea.

The set menus offer a veritable feast of the best of British food, almost too much to eat, and the vegetarian menu does not compromise in any way. The savoury courses on both not only include a variety of innovative sandwich fillings served in delicious breads, ranging from rye, tomato, beetroot, and onion, but there is also a selection

ADDRESS: 8th floor, OXO Tower, Barge House Street, South Bank, London SE1 9PH

TEL: +44 (0)20 7803 3888

EMAIL: oxo.reservations@harveynichols.com

WEB: www.oxotowerrestaurant.com

AFTERNOON TEA SERVED: Monday to Friday 3.00pm–4.30pm, Saturday 3.00pm–4.00pm, Sunday 3.45pm–4.45pm

SET TEAS: traditional, children's tea. Vegetarian and gluten-free options available.

NEAREST UNDERGROUND/ MAINLINE STATIONS: Southwark, Blackfriars, Waterloo, Embankment, Temple

PLACES OF INTEREST NEARBY: Globe Theatre, Tate Britain, South Bank Centre, Mermaid Theatre, National Theatre, BFI Southbank, St Paul's Cathedral, River Thames, Thames riverside walkway, Victoria Embankment Gardens, Coin Street specialist shops, galleries, and design studios

of mini bites, accompanied by variety of condiments. Non-vegetarians should eat the Scotch quail's egg with smoked salmon first, whilst the inside yolk is still runny; vegetarians, whose quail's egg is wrapped in spinach and enclosed in a crispy coated case, should do likewise. The yummy mini Yorkshire puddings are filled with either beef or bubble and squeak, and the little choux buns with crab meat or houmous,. Then, when you have tackled Penny's tasty scones, slathered with gorgeous preserves and clotted cream, you still have the seasonally changing pastries and miniature dessert to eat, but they are just the right size to finish with. The British feel is carried through to the tea list, for the selection on offer is all produced by Tregothnan, a small Cornish company who pioneered the first tea plantations in the country.

A special menu for those under twelve hits just the right note with a shot glass of banana milkshake, finger sandwiches with traditional fillings, and small, enticing bites like caramel and sea salt popcorn. Mini scones are complete

with clotted cream and jam, and no doubt the adults will be eyeing up the caramel cream éclair and white and dark chocolate brownie. For drinks there is a babyccino, milky tea, or a raspberry and rhubarb iced tea. This specially-created menu comes complete with coloured pencils and colouring books, so there is no time for the little darlings to be bored or distract you from your own lovely tea.

THE PETERSHAM

When you arrive at The Petersham, you can't help but be struck by the imposing building, with its turrets and tower, balconies, and high-pitched roofs. Inside, the hall is dominated by a magnificent, unsupported Portland stone staircase, reputedly the tallest one of its kind in the country. As if the architectural features were not enough, the view from the restaurant, across the historic Petersham Meadows to the famous bend in the River Thames, is unparalleled. The atmosphere here is warm and welcoming, and afternoon tea has become somewhat of an institution over the years. You can expect a traditional menu with a twist to the scones, pastries, and cakes, depending on the theme when you visit. The great river and the spectacular annual race that takes place in September provide the inspiration for the Thames afternoon tea. Wimbledon, the Chelsea Flower Show, Mother's Day, and more all get

ADDRESS: Nightingale Lane, Richmond, Surrey TW10 6UZ

TEL: +44 (0)20 8939 1084

EMAIL: enq@petershamhotel.co.uk

WEB: www.petershamhotel.co.uk /restaurant/afternoon-tea

AFTERNOON TEA SERVED:
Monday to Saturday
3.00pm–5.30pm,
Sunday 4.00pm–5.30pm,
Boxing Day 1.00pm–6.00pm

SET TEAS: depending on the time of year, traditional, Wimbledon, Chelsea Flower Show, Christmas, and other special occasion teas. Gluten free available with 24 hours' notice.

NEAREST UNDERGROUND/ MAINLINE STATIONS: Richmond

PLACES OF INTEREST NEARBY: Kew Gardens, Ham House and gardens, River Thames, Historic Richmond, Richmond Park, Syon Park, Petersham Nurseries

celebrated, and, come December, the festive menu has winter treats such as cranberry and lemon scones, Christmas cupcakes, and classic gingerbread. You'll always find fruitcake and a chocolate and hazelnut Opera cake on the menu, for they are favourites amongst the regular guests. When it comes to the liquid refreshment, there is fine Petersham champagne and a small list of excellent leaf teas from Novus Teas to choose from. Tea service follows lunch, so if you arrive early, there may be some people still lingering over coffee, but every guest is important here, and you can be sure that you will be well looked after. The memory of the view, and of the tasty, generous afternoon tea, will linger long after you have left.

THE RITZ

The Palm Court

César Ritz's gracious Edwardian hotel has been an icon in the heart of Mayfair since 1906 and can count amongst its famous patrons the Prince of Wales (the future King Edward VII), Anna Pavlova, the Aga Khan, Paul Getty, and Winston Churchill. At the heart of the hotel is the world-famous Palm Court, lavishly decorated and gilded, a wonderful space that is the epitome of sophistication and elegance. As you go up the few marble stairs from the ground floor central gallery area and pass between a pair of grand marbled columns, you know that there is a real treat in store. Pretty Louis XVI chairs and marble-topped tables beautifully set with crisp linen and delicate 'Ritz' bone china await the guests eager to share in what is a quintessentially Ritz experience.

ADDRESS: 150 Piccadilly, St James's, London W1J 9BR

TEL: +44 (0)20 7300 2345

EMAIL: tea@theritzlondon.com

WEB: www.theritzlondon.com

AFTERNOON TEA SERVED: daily at 11.30am, 1.30pm, 3.30pm, 5.30pm, 7.30pm

SET TEAS: traditional, champagne, Celebration Tea (with or without champagne), seasonal teas including Valentine's Day, Mother's Day, and Christmas, children's tea (up to the age of 15). See the website for seasonal special offers. Dietary requirements can be catered for with advance notice.

DRESS CODE: gentlemen are required to wear a jacket and tie (jeans and sportswear are not permitted for either ladies or gentlemen) for afternoon tea in The Palm Court

NEAREST UNDERGROUND STATIONS: Green Park

PLACES OF INTEREST NEARBY: Royal Academy of Arts, Green Park, Saville Row, Burlington Arcade, Bond Street, Fortnum & Mason

There is plenty of time to settle down, take in the buzzy atmosphere, and tune in to the delicate strains of the resident pianist, harpist, or string quintet whilst your waiter helps you select your tea from the 18 splendid varieties of leaf tea on offer. All of them, including the exclusive Ritz Royal Blend, are sourced worldwide by the Ritz's certified Tea Sommelier. Afternoon tea here follows the best British traditions. On the lower tier of your cake stand, you have a generous selection of elegant sandwiches, made using a variety of different breads. For example, you could enjoy sourdough for the smoked salmon, granary for the cucumber, and tomato bread for the cheddar cheese and chutney. Your server will be more than happy to replenish any or all of the varieties you choose.

It's up to you whether you have the scones next – delivered warm from the oven, and served with Devonshire clotted cream and strawberry preserve – or prefer to indulge first in the delectable afternoon tea pastries on the top tier. The selection changes and might include a raspberry and rosewater macaron, a miniature chocolate and hazelnut sponge, and a choux bun filled with crème pâtissière. The finale is a slice of cake, a choice between, perhaps, a strawberry sponge and a coconut and exotic fruit cake, served from the cake trolley.

For that extra touch, your afternoon tea can be accompanied by a glass of the Ritz's own Brut or Rosé champagne, and if your visit is for a special occasion, then why not order a cake to complete the celebration? The pianist will be delighted to play happy birthday whilst you blow out the candles, marking the highlight of a very special experience. And if you should happen to be planning a visit between late November and the 30th of December, you'll find the Palm Court transformed into a winter wonderland, with a lavishly decorated Christmas tree centre stage and the Ritz choir singing carols. Add some warm mince pies and the Ritz Christmas Spice tea to the menu, and you are in for an unforgettable time.

ROSEWOOD LONDON
The Mirror Room

As you pass through the central carriageway entrance and dome into the grand courtyard, you exchange the bustle of High Holborn for the calm sanctuary of Rosewood London, which from 1914 until the 1960s was the headquarters of the Pearl Assurance Company. This is a truly remarkable Edwardian edifice which has been lovingly restored, and whilst much of its heritage has been carefully retained, it has been brought up to date in magnificent style. The beguiling jewel box design of the Mirror Room, tucked away in the heart of the hotel, is the perfect setting for the Rosewood's truly contemporary Art Afternoon Tea. Floor to ceiling mirrors create a feeling of space and recall the glittering jewels that ladies of a bygone era wore when they took tea. Lounge-style seating, tables laid with crisp linen runners, fine Limoges porcelain, silverware, and sparkling crystal set the scene. It's a relaxed but refined all-day dining room where you can enjoy good service and the special Art Afternoon Tea, which features pastries inspired by well-known artists whose work is exhibited in London, from Banksy and Mark Rothko to Damien Hirst and Alexander Calder. But first you will enjoy delicious traditional sandwiches and a choice of scones served with clotted cream, strawberry jam, and lemon curd. A fine tea cellar lists white, black, yellow, green,

oolong, pu-erh, and herbal leaf teas, so there is something to please everyone. Leave as you entered, across the grand Edwardian courtyard and back onto the bustling High Holborn.

ADDRESS: 252 High Holborn, Holborn, London WC1V 7EN

TEL: +44 (0)20 3747 8620

EMAIL: mirrorroom@rosewoodhotels.com

WEB: www.rosewoodhotels.com /en/london

OFFERS: see www.afternoontea .co.uk/uk/london

AFTERNOON TEA SERVED: Monday to Friday 2.00pm–6.00pm, Saturday and Sunday 12.00pm–7.00pm

SET TEAS: Art Afternoon Tea

DRESS CODE: smart casual

NEAREST UNDERGROUND STATIONS: Holborn

PLACES OF INTEREST NEARBY: British Museum, Sir John Soane Museum, Lincoln's Inn Fields, Charles Dickens Museum, The London Silver Vaults, Hunterian Museum, Royal College of Surgeons, Conway Hall

THE RUBENS
AT THE PALACE

*B*race yourself for a right royal treat at the Rubens at the Palace, a very traditional English hotel with a rich history. Long before it became a member of the Red Carnation Collection of hotels, it was known as the Hotel Rubens, and during the Second World War served as the headquarters of the Polish government-in-exile. Now it's a luxury hotel where personal service is of paramount importance. Afternoon tea is served in the Palace Lounge, with its regal red furnishings and carpet. The staff in reception will direct you to the lounge, which is reached either through the dining room or the bar, and from here you have an unparalleled view of the comings and goings of the Royal Mews immediately opposite. This is where State vehicles, including royal horse-drawn carriages and motorcars, are housed, providing road transport for the Queen and members of the Royal family.

ADDRESS: 39 Buckingham Palace Road, Westminster, London SW1W 0PS

TEL: +44 (0)20 7834 6600

WEB: www.rubenshotel.com

AFTERNOON TEA SERVED: Monday to Friday 2.00pm–4.30pm, Saturday and Sunday 1.00pm–5.00pm

SET TEAS: Royal Afternoon Tea, Prince and Princess Royal Tea (for children under 12). A range of dietary requirements can be catered for, preferably with advance notice.

NEAREST UNDERGROUND STATIONS: Victoria, St James's Park, Hyde Park Corner

PLACES OF INTEREST NEARBY: The Royal Mews, Buckingham Palace, The Queen's Gallery, Green Park

Start with a glass of champagne whilst you peruse the menu, and let the staff introduce you to the Twinings teas on offer, including one called The Full English, just the ticket for those who like a really strong cuppa. Tuck into first-rate sandwiches, including stalwarts like cucumber or egg and cress, as well as the very delicious coronation chicken, rolled in toasted flaked almonds, and, for a real change, Arbroath Smokie with chive mayonnaise. The orange-scented scones, served with citrus curd, are deliciously different, and the plain ones are equally good accompanied by preserves and clotted cream. Royalty is celebrated in the regularly changing menu of pastries, with the likes of a Coronation tart with pistachio and raspberry and a diamond chocolate biscuit cake with chocolate mousse. To complete the treat, enjoy a rather nice fruit posset served in a shot glass – if it's plum, it will be topped with blood orange caviar, giving a burst of flavour. All in all, it's a generous tea, beautifully served, and a fitting way to end a day of royal visits.

Brazil Nut Cake

Recipe courtesy of The Rubens at the Palace

INGREDIENTS

- 500 g (3½ cups) whole Brazil nuts
- 500 g (2¼ cups) dates, pitted and halved
- 150 g (⅔ cup) candied cherries
- 150 g (1¼ cups) plain (all-purpose) flour
- 150 g (⅔ cup) sugar
- 3 g (½ tsp.) salt
- 2 g (½ tsp.) baking powder
- 3 eggs
- 1 tsp. vanilla extract

Bea Tollman is President and Founder of the boutique Red Carnation Hotel Collection, which also includes The Milestone Hotel and Egerton House Hotel. This recipe is from her cookbook *A Life in Food*. Serves 8.

METHOD

1. In a large bowl, combine the nuts, dates, and cherries. Sift the flour, sugar, salt, and baking powder over the nut mixture and mix thoroughly.
2. Beat the eggs until foamy, add the vanilla, and then stir into the fruit and nut mixture, mixing well.
3. Grease and double-line a 24 cm x 6 cm x 1 cm (9.5 inch x 2.5 inch x 0.5 inch or similar) loaf tin (pan) with parchment paper, then pour in the mix, spreading evenly.
4. Bake at about 170°C (338°F) for 1½ hours.
5. Remove the tin (pan) from the oven. When cool, loosen the edges with a knife and remove the cake from the tin (pan).

This recipe presents terms and measurements for both UK and US readers. Units are given first for UK readers in the original measurement units, then for US readers in converted units in parentheses. Do not mix the units. US equivalent terms are also given in parentheses where needed.

SANCTUM SOHO HOTEL
Wild Heart Restaurant

*O*f the two set afternoon tea menus on offer at Sanctum Soho, the Gents Afternoon Tea certainly has something different to offer, and could stand a hungry man or woman in good stead as late lunch or early supper. The boutique hotel is secreted behind the façade of two Georgian townhouses, and the Wild Heart restaurant is a terrific venue full of vintage glamour with oak floors, a dazzling bar, and gold leather banquette seating providing private enclaves in which to meet friends, discuss business, or just party. Other than a steaming pot of tea, and with the exception of the delicious scones, the Gents Afternoon Tea is a departure from tradition and is a carnivore's dream. Start with a Scotch egg and a ham hock with piccalilli, followed by a mini steak roll and a mini burger. If this is not enough, then you can tuck into an oyster served with a

ADDRESS: 20 Warwick Street,
Soho, London W1B 5NF

TEL: +44 (0)20 7292 6102

EMAIL: no.20@sanctumsoho.com

WEB: www.sanctumsoho.com

AFTERNOON TEA SERVED:
Monday to Friday and Sunday
3.00pm–5.00pm, Saturday
4.00pm–6.00pm. Advance
booking required, with a deposit.
The hotel operates a 72-hour
cancellation policy.

SET TEAS: Gents Afternoon Tea,
Ladies High Heels Tea

**NEAREST UNDERGROUND
STATIONS:** Piccadilly Circus

**PLACES OF INTEREST
NEARBY:** Regent Street, Soho

champagne glass vinegar foam, as well as baby back ribs that are flame grilled and served with barbecue sauce. In deference to tradition, there are indeed scones, but they come studded with raisins and laced with rum and are accompanied by clotted cream and homemade jam. Then there is still dessert to follow – a chocolate brownie with a malt Chantilly cream. Finally, if you want to move up to the fifth-floor roof terrace, you can sup a tankard of Jack Daniels' Gentleman's Jack and smoke the Villager Export cigar, completing your experience. All is not lost if you happen to be accompanying a man to tea here, for the ladies can order the Ladies High Heels Tea. Enjoy a glass of bubbling Prosecco with your ladylike sandwiches, slather the plain and fruit scones with clotted cream and jam, and then tuck in to a selection of mini sweets. For the finale, there are strawberries and cream. Sanctum Soho successfully blends tradition with cutting edge, quirky style, and the menus, especially the Gents Afternoon Tea, are strikingly innovative.

SANDERSON

*F*ortunately there is no need to go down the rabbit hole to enjoy this fairytale experience – you just have to join in the fun. This quirky afternoon tea would thrill Alice of Wonderland fame and have prompted her to say 'curiouser and curiouser' as she embarked on her tea adventure. The menu is secreted inside a vintage book, the linen napkins have a paper riddle wrapped around them, and the sugar cubes are hidden inside a charming musical box topped by a twirling ballerina. Choose from one of Sanderson's Alice-inspired exclusive teas, served in a china teapot adorned with kings and queens, and dine off sandwich plates featuring zebras, birdcages, carousels, and ticking clocks. The food, which varies seasonally, is whimsical, from the 'strawberries and cream' homemade marshmallow mushrooms to the Mad Hatter's tiny 'lost' carrot and fennel meringues served on a bed of pea shoots. The White Rabbit cucumber sandwich and King of Hearts croque-monsieur stack vie for space on the bottom of the stand with a crisp-coated smoked salmon Scotch quail's egg and a Cornish crab bridge roll. Next up are the warm scones served with clotted cream and a choice of fruit preserves. There's no chance of losing the Alice theme when it comes

ADDRESS: 50 Berners Street, Fitzrovia, London W1T 3NG

TEL: +44 (0)20 7300 5588

WEB: www.sandersonlondon.com

AFTERNOON TEA SERVED:
Monday to Saturday
12.30pm–4.00pm,
Sunday 1.00pm–5.00pm.
Evening tea served daily
7.00pm–9.00pm, with age
restriction 21+.

SET TEAS: Mad Hatter's
Afternoon Tea, Mad Hatter's Tipsy
Evening Tea

**NEAREST UNDERGROUND
STATIONS:** Tottenham Court
Road, Goodge Street

**PLACES OF INTEREST
NEARBY:** Soho, Oxford Street

to the sweet course – the Queen of Hearts appears as a jammy dodger, the March Hare, always worrying about the time, has a vanilla pocket-watch macaron, and Tweedle Dee gets a look in with lemon curd financier. Extras include amusingly named cocktails which remind you of some of the nonsense in *Alice's Adventures in Wonderland*, like 'the Caucus Race

and a Long Tale', or you can choose champagnes to complete the occasion. This is an unusual tea which delights children and adults alike and is certain to make you grin like the Cheshire cat.

The Mad Hatter's Tipsy Evening Tea makes a refreshing change when the evenings are longer, it stays light later, and you can unwind in the lush surroundings of the courtyard garden. Start with the savoury course, delight in the sweet treats, sip Alice's bottle of 'drink me' potion (a concoction of orange and Cointreau), and, finally, enjoy the flight of four cocktails, including a mini Kir Royale and a mini martini.

THE SAVOY

The Thames Foyer

As you descend the elegant staircase to the Thames Foyer of the Grade II listed Savoy hotel, you can't help but notice an aura of restrained elegance and grandeur. Often described as 'the vibrant heart of the hotel', the foyer was built into the centre of the original 1889 building when the Savoy was extended in 1904. After the completion of a stylish refurbishment in 2010, light once again floods in from the great glass cupola above you, and music played by the resident pianist drifts across the room. The tranquil ambience is complemented by the discreet but attentive service, and guests may linger in the sofas and armchairs, or at their table, for as long as they like.

ADDRESS: Strand, Covent Garden, London WC2R 0EU

TEL: +44 (0)20 7420 2111

EMAIL: savoy@fairmont.com

WEB: www.fairmont.com/savoy

AFTERNOON TEA SERVED: daily 1.00pm–5.45pm. Advance reservations highly recommended.

SET TEAS: traditional, Traditional High Tea, seasonal teas, Christmas tea. Food allergies and special dietary requirements can be catered for with advance notice.

DRESS CODE: smart casual; no sportswear

NEAREST UNDERGROUND STATIONS: Covent Garden, Embankment, Charing Cross

PLACES OF INTEREST NEARBY: Somerset House, The Courtauld Gallery and Institute of Art, Royal Festival Hall, National Theatre, Savoy Theatre, Covent Garden, Royal Opera House, Transport Museum, London Film Museum, Cinema Museum

The selection of finger sandwiches on brown, olive, white, and herb and spinach bread have various vegetarian, fish, and meat fillings, and all are readily replenished. The perfectly glazed, warm plain and raisin scones are served with Cornish clotted cream and both homemade lemon curd and strawberry preserve. Amongst the delicate afternoon tea pastries, you'll probably find a delectable coffee and hazelnut éclair, a tartlet of crisp shortcrust pastry filled with raspberry bavarois and vanilla-scented cream, and a strawberry macaron, and that is before you are presented with your choice from the Thames Foyer signature cakes – possibly Victoria sponge or banana and milk chocolate cake. For those with a bigger appetite, the high

tea is wonderful, for it combines the major elements of the traditional afternoon tea with a savoury course. Follow the traditional menu as far as the pastries, which are replaced by a platter of crayfish and green asparagus with a poached egg and lemon hollandaise. Return to a sweet course for the finale – two individual Thames Foyer signature cakes.

Connoisseurs of tea will be spoilt for choice, as the Savoy offers a distinctive collection of leaf teas. Besides their own special breakfast and afternoon blends, there are two fine and rare teas – Iron Buddha Oolong and the definitive Japanese Wazuka Sencha – plus two flowering teas, white and green teas, scented white and green teas, black scented or flavoured teas, decaffeinated teas, and a selection of herbal and fruit infusions. You can see that tea is taken very seriously here. Before you leave, you might like to pay a visit to the in-house shop, Savoy Tea, where you can purchase any of the teas in specially designed caddies, another pastry to take home, or a piece of bespoke tea crockery designed by Wedgwood. Pure extravagance.

SKETCH

*Y*ou'll find sketch secreted away behind the façade of an elegant 18th-century building in Conduit Street, Mayfair, just a stone's throw from Regent Street, the road named in honour of the Prince Regent by the distinguished architect John Nash. The interior will appeal to lovers of the eclectic, for it is a unique destination for food, art, and music. Afternoon tea is generally served in The Gallery, so-called because of the walls lined with David Shrigley's original and witty drawings. They provide a striking backdrop to the unashamedly pink, plush décor of the space, an extravagant room furnished with pink banquette seating where the champagne trolley is pink and every piece of china has a humorous message inscribed on it.

The French chefs at sketch have created their own version of a classic afternoon tea, and occasionally produce a very special seasonal

ADDRESS: 9 Conduit Street, Mayfair, London W1S 2XG

TEL: +44 (0)20 7659 4500

EMAIL: info@sketch.london

WEB: www.sketch.london

AFTERNOON TEA SERVED: daily 11.30am–4.00pm

SET TEAS: cream tea, traditional tea, champagne tea, children's tea

NEAREST UNDERGROUND STATIONS: Oxford Circus, Bond Street, Piccadilly

PLACES OF INTEREST NEARBY: Bond Street, Regent Street, Royal Academy, Oxford Street

version. The little darlings in your party can enjoy a specially tailored feast and go home with their own Pat the Bear. Since your cup of tea is central to the event, the resident Tea Master has sourced leaves from across the globe, bringing the very finest teas from a range of black, oolong, white, green, pu-erh, and herbal for you to choose from. To add some fizz, you could enjoy a glass of Pommery Brut Silver or Brut Rosé champagne, or a glass of fine English sparkling wine. For those who prefer a non-alcoholic celebratory drink, there is a fruit-packed raspberry Bellini as well as white or rosé sparkling grape juice.

Now on to the food. Starting with a trip down memory lane is the sketch version of toast soldiers and a soft-boiled egg, only in this case, the egg white is replaced with a flavoursome béchamel cheese sauce. As you dip in your bread, the caviar man – probably in a

pink suit – is likely to arrive with his pot of caviar, ready to serve you a teaspoonful of rich, creamy Oscietra caviar, the eggs just waiting to burst in your mouth. Amongst the sandwiches, you can expect coronation chicken, smoked salmon, and egg mayonnaise topped with caviar and a quail's egg. A choice of organic strawberry and fig jam accompany the sultana and plain scones, and in case you are unsure what to do with the clotted cream, *Debrett's Guide to Etiquette* declares that jam comes first. The selection of petits gateaux combine tradition with innovation, from the chef's own take on Battenberg cake to the tangy Lincolnshire rhubarb cheesecake to the Malabar Marshmallow, which evokes memories of a classic bubblegum flavour dating back more than fifty years. The finale, if you have the space, is a piece of cake from the trolley, a fitting end to an afternoon spent enjoying fine food in fun surroundings.

SOFITEL LONDON ST JAMES
The Rose Lounge

Situated right on the corner of Waterloo Place and St James, the Sofitel London St James is hidden behind a stunning neo-classical façade. The Grade II listed building, dating back to 1923, has an illustrious past and, like so many of London's grand edifices, served as a bank, and was also once occupied by Cox & Company, the world's longest-established travel agents. Since 2002, the building has been home to an elegant, sophisticated hotel. As one might expect, the Rose Lounge, where afternoon tea is most frequently served, has more than a touch of pink about it, from the deep rose of the settees, to the pale rose marble table-tops, to the pretty pink Bernardaud porcelain teaware. The lounge retains the impression of a comfortable room in a private home, with seating arranged in discrete conversation spaces. Whenever you visit you'll be serenaded by the gentle strings of a harp, and if you

ADDRESS: 6 Waterloo Place, St James's, London SW1Y 4AN

TEL: +44 (0)20 7747 2238

EMAIL: H3144-FB10@sofitel.com

WEB: www.sofitelstjames.com

AFTERNOON TEA SERVED: daily 12.00pm–6.00pm

SET TEAS: Le Tea en Rose, with champagne options; Le Goûter (children's tea)

NEAREST UNDERGROUND STATIONS: Piccadilly Circus

PLACES OF INTEREST NEARBY: Green Park, St James's Park, St James's Palace, Pall Mall, Horse Guards Parade, Institute of Contemporary Arts, Trafalgar Square, National Gallery, National Portrait Gallery, Royal Society, British Academy

have a special musical request, the harpist is more than happy to oblige. Very pleasant and discrete staff take you through the tea and menu options, which have a definite French touch about them. You'll be served with a smoothie to start, followed by sandwiches and savouries, and there is always a vegetarian option. The scones are excellent, served with clotted cream, lemon curd, and a delicate rose-scented strawberry jam. You get to choose your patisseries from the trolley, and whilst these change on a regular basis, there is always a raspberry macaron, and very often an opera cake and an apricot and pistachio tart. In addition, there are special cakes made for Mother's Day and Christmas. There is also a smashing tailor-made afternoon tea for children, with finger sandwiches, a variety of cakes, and fresh fruit, all served in an artist's paint box along with a colouring kit.

The teas are supplied by Dammann Frères, whose history can be traced back to Louis XIV, who granted Monsieur Damame the exclusive privilege to sell tea in France in 1692. The list, which includes some rare and seasonal

teas, also has two related to roses. Rose Buds is a delicate infusion with a subtle rose flavor and which looks magical in the clear glass teapots, and Bulgare is a subtle and sensuous herbal tea which has a delicate lemony scent and a fruity taste. There is, of course, a champagne option, including an hour and a half of free-flowing bubbly. As an alternative, you could have the deliciously decadent Edgerton Pink Gin Signature Cocktail, which gets its pink tinge not from fruity raspberries or roses, but from pomegranate extract. A slightly modified Rose Lounge afternoon tea menu is also served in the beautiful Balcon restaurant, and is a good place to sit if you are a party of guests. C'est magnifique.

THE SOHO HOTEL

*S*ituated just around the corner from Soho Square in a quiet mews off buzzing, busy Dean Street, with its connection to the film industry, the Soho Hotel is as surprising as it is sophisticated, spacious, and incredibly stylish. The décor is a quirky mix of traditional English furniture and vibrant modern fabrics, with an eclectic display of artworks adorning the walls. If you like to be in a space humming with activity, then ask for a table in the Refuel bar and restaurant. For a more peaceful, relaxing ambience, you can ask to be seated in the elegant drawing room – not guaranteed though – with its hugely inviting sofas, or in the comfort of the wood-panelled library. Whichever innovative set afternoon tea is on offer, you can be sure it will be wonderful. It might be traditional, with delicious finger sandwiches, super scones, essential clotted cream and jam, and delectable cakes; or it might be the

ADDRESS: 4 Richmond Mews,
Soho, London W1D 3DH

TEL: +44 (0)20 7559 3007

EMAIL: refuel@sohohotel.com

WEB: www.firmdalehotels.com
/hotels/london/the-soho-hotel

AFTERNOON TEA SERVED:
daily 12.00pm–5.00pm

SET TEAS: traditional (periodically
replaced with a special seasonal
tea), champagne, Film Club with
afternoon tea. Reduced sugar, gluten-
free, or vegan options available, please
order in advance.

**NEAREST UNDERGROUND
STATIONS:** Tottenham Court
Road, Oxford Circus

**PLACES OF INTEREST
NEARBY:** Oxford Street,
Bloomsbury, British Museum,
Soho Square, French Protestant
(Huguenot) Church of London,
Golden Square, Soho and Chinatown

champagne tea, with the addition of smoked
salmon blinis and a bowl of strawberries; or it
could be G & Tea, inspired by gin botanicals
and served with a special cocktail as well as the
food menu. For a fabulous treat, why not book
seats for the Film Club, watch the movie of the
week in one of the state-of-the-art screening
rooms, and then enjoy a blissful afternoon tea
in the restaurant? This is somewhere where you
could really spend the whole day.

ST MARTINS LANE

The Den

*L*ocated just off the front lobby of this stylish boutique hotel in the heart of London's theatreland, what at first sight looks like a classically furnished and decorated English gentleman's oak-panelled club room turns out to be full of surprises. In the Den, the talking point has to be the art on the walls, which is eccentric, quirky, and slightly surreal. When you've taken this in, you'll see there are books begging to be read and backgammon tables waiting for you to begin a game. Add to this comfy leather sofas and warm lighting, and you are set for a very relaxed afternoon. If you happen to be visiting in the summer months, you could enquire about taking tea on the terrace.

The fine bone china, aptly named Rosie Lee – rhyming Cockney slang for 'tea' – is designed by Ted Baker, and is a modern, playful

ADDRESS: 45 St Martin's Lane, Covent Garden, London WC2N 4HX

TEL: +44 (0)20 7300 5500

WEB: www.morganshotelgroup.com

AFTERNOON TEA SERVED: daily 12.00pm–5.00pm

SET TEAS: options include a gin and tonic or champagne addition. For special dietary requirements, please notify in advance.

NEAREST UNDERGROUND STATIONS: Leicester Square, Charing Cross

PLACES OF INTEREST NEARBY: Trafalgar Square, National Portrait Gallery, National Gallery, Theatreland, Covent Garden

take on a vintage floral tea set. You can't but help enjoy the food, which combines savoury and sweet items. Menus change regularly, so the first course might include a delicious brioche with brie, mushrooms, garlic, and parsley, olive and chilli bread with smoked salmon, and a caraway roll with a delicate chicken, tarragon, lime, and sundried tomato filling. When you have had enough of this course, enjoy a very satisfying scone, accompanied by jam and clotted cream. You may need a rest before moving on to the sweet treats, and there is no place for counting calories here, nor is there a rush, so take your time as you enjoy the varied pastries. You will be able to choose your tea from a small, select list of leaf tea from master tea blenders Harney and Sons – unless you fancy something stronger. In that case, the bar team has created a special Gin & Tonic menu, inspired by the off-kilter artwork on the walls, with each drink reflecting an element of the portraits. It's a refreshing way to wash down the delicious tea and help you to feel relaxed and replete.

ST PANCRAS
RENAISSANCE HOTEL
Hansom Lounge

ccupying the former cobbled driveway where hansom cabs once deposited their well-heeled passengers, Hansom Lounge at St Pancras Renaissance Hotel combines Victorian splendour with contemporary style. Flanked on either side by the window bays of the original station and hotel walls, and vaulted by its high glazed roof and Barlow Blue girders, the space is as dramatic by day as it is by night. The hotel, designed by Sir Gilbert Scott, is an architectural masterpiece, and the lounge is both a spectacular hotel lobby and meeting place, with designated seating for afternoon tea. You'll find the savoury element of the menu is not too traditional, with brioche, cranberry, brown, and onion breads instead of the more familiar white bread, and several meat fillings along with vegetarian and seafood fillings. Any of these will be replaced without fuss to suit your dietary preferences. The blueberry and white

ADDRESS: Euston Road, Kings Cross, London NW1 2AR

TEL: +44 (0)20 7841 3540

EMAIL: bookingoffice@renaissancehotels.com

WEB: www.stpancraslondon.com

AFTERNOON TEA SERVED: daily 1.30pm–5.00pm

SET TEAS: traditional, St Pancras Afternoon Tea (which includes an alcoholic drink of choice)

NEAREST UNDERGROUND STATIONS: King's Cross

PLACES OF INTEREST NEARBY: The British Library, The Wellcome Collection, The Society of Friends, King's Place, King's Cross

chocolate scones are equally novel, followed by innovative sweets, featuring salted caramel macarons and a sticky toffee pudding in a glass. Of course the menus do change according to the season, so variations may occur. Besides the option of champagne, why not try one of the Hansom Lounge's unique drinks, which include The Fencer, Purple Heart, Chambers Club, and the Tsar Alexander, all designed to complement the flavours of the food. There is a list of fine teas to choose from, completing the occasion, and you'll be sure to leave fortified to face the rest of the day.

THE STAFFORD

The Game Bird

*I*f you are looking for somewhere unexpected in the heart of London where you can enjoy a quiet afternoon tea in elegant surroundings, then look no further than The Game Bird at the Stafford. Tucked away in a cul-de-sac off St James's, the hotel is an oasis of calm just moments from Piccadilly and Green Park. Originally built as private residences in the 17th century, the Stafford can claim to be one of the oldest hotels near Buckingham Palace, and is a clever blend of Victorian grandeur and modern comfort. The hotel celebrated its centenary in 2012 and boasts a fascinating history, which includes its use as a club for American and Canadian officers during the Second World War, whilst the wine cellars were used as air raid shelters. Afternoon tea here has all the hallmarks of a quintessentially English occasion, where guests can relax and unwind in the elegant drawing rooms that interconnect with the restaurant.

ADDRESS: 16–18 St James's Place, St James's, London SW1A 1NJ

TEL: +44 (0)20 7493 0111

EMAIL: reservations@thestaffordlondon.com

WEB: www.thestaffordlondon.com

AFTERNOON TEA SERVED: daily 12.00pm–7.00pm

SET TEAS: cream tea, traditional tea

NEAREST UNDERGROUND STATIONS: Green Park

PLACES OF INTEREST NEARBY: Green Park, Buckingham Palace, St James's Palace, Royal Academy of Arts, Bond Street shopping, Piccadilly

On weekends, and depending on the weather, you can take advantage of one of London's best-kept secrets, and have your tea al fresco in the charming private courtyard that adjoins the American Bar. Wherever you are seated, you will be served a very traditional tea of finger sandwiches on brown and white breads (with vegetarian options available as required), raisin and plain scones with lashings of clotted cream and jam, dainty seasonal patisserie, and crisp puff pastry Eccles cakes. There is a good selection of tea from Camellia's Tea House, cocktails if you prefer, and champagne for that extra special celebration. You may be spoilt for choice in this prestigious part of London, but the Stafford certainly offers tranquillity and gentility.

THE WALLACE RESTAURANT

hat more stunning venue could there be for tea in the heart of London than The Wallace, the restaurant situated in the beautiful Sculpture Garden of Hertford House, home to the world-famous Wallace Art Collection? The historic London townhouse, originally known as Manchester House, was built between 1776–1788 for the 4th Duke of Manchester because, believe it or not, there was good duck shooting nearby. It then served as the Spanish Embassy before being leased to the 2nd Marquess of Hertford. For a time, in the mid-1800s, it was home to the French Embassy, before the 4th Marquess of Hertford's illegitimate son moved back to London, bringing with him his massive art collection to add to the treasures already there. The house first opened as a public museum in 1900, and the central courtyard, transformed in 2000 by the

ADDRESS: Hertford House, Manchester Square, Marylebone, London W1U 3BN

TEL: +44 (0)20 7563 9505

EMAIL: reservations@thewallace restaurant.com

WEB: www.peytonandbyrne.co.uk /wallace-restaurant

AFTERNOON TEA SERVED: daily 2.30pm–4.30pm

SET TEAS: English Afternoon Tea, a la carte

NEAREST UNDERGROUND STATIONS: Bond Street, Baker Street

PLACES OF INTEREST NEARBY: Wallace Collection, Bond Street, Oxford Street

installation of a fabulous glass atrium roof, is now home to the Sculpture Gallery and the informal but elegant French brasserie-style Wallace restaurant.

As you make your way in to have tea, you can't help but notice the wonderful paintings by artists such as Titian, Rembrandt, Hals (The Laughing Cavalier), and Velázquez. This is a positively charming, light and bright place to while away an hour or so, seated at tables amongst beautiful trees beneath the glass roof. The set afternoon tea menu is an affordable, classic English one, with traditional smoked salmon and cream cheese, cucumber and dill, egg mayonnaise, and coronation chicken sandwiches served on Peyton and Byrne brown and white breads. There are nice scones, jam, and clotted cream, plus a regularly changing selection of mini-cakes. Add your choice of tea from the list of more than 20 loose-leaf teas on offer – including favourites like Darjeeling and Assam and the more unusual China White Silver needles – and maybe a glass of champagne, and you are all set for a last look at the exquisite art collection on your way out. If you plan properly, you can take in one of the free tours as well.

THE WELLESLEY, KNIGHTSBRIDGE

The Jazz Lounge

*A*s you approach the entrance to The Wellesley, spare a moment to stand back and look at the lower façade of the building and the terracotta tiled arches and entranceway: somewhat surprisingly, this building, designed by architect Leslie Green, began life in 1906 as Hyde Park Corner underground station. It went from station to smart 1920s London townhouse, and then for another three decades the basement was home to Pizza on the Park, one of London's best-known jazz venues. In fact the interior has been designed to recapture the feel of the 1920s and 30s. The décor in the Jazz Lounge, where afternoon tea is served, pays homage to the jazz era and to the art deco style of the period. It's an elegant and comfortable mirrored room with crystal chandeliers where the pianist plays every day and will happily respond to any request you may have. Tables are set with crisp white linen, fine china designed

ADDRESS: 11 Knightsbridge, Belgravia, London SW1X 7LY

TEL: +44 (0)20 3668 6530

EMAIL: restaurant@thewellesley.co.uk

WEB: www.thewellesley.co.uk

OFFERS: see www.afternoontea .co.uk/uk/london

AFTERNOON TEA SERVED: Monday to Friday 3.00pm–5.00pm, Saturday and Sunday 2.00pm–6.30pm

SET TEAS: traditional. Occasional themed menus available.

NEAREST UNDERGROUND STATIONS: Hyde Park Corner

PLACES OF INTEREST NEARBY: Hyde Park, Apsley House, Knightsbridge, Harrods

exclusively for the hotel by William Edwards, and fresh flowers.

If you have pushed the boat out and are sipping champagne – either Brut, Rosé, or the magnificent Krug Grande Cuvée – you'll also be enjoying the fresh strawberries and cream that accompany the glass of bubbly. Outside of the occasional themed afternoon teas – one celebrated Winston Churchill and showcased filo pastry cannoli cigars with a dark chocolate mousse, and a pastry that resembled his signature bowler hat – expect delightfully tasty, well-filled finger sandwiches and miniature savouries, good scones, and a nice selection of sweet treats, including a take on the traditional Battenberg cake. Exotic teas have been hand-selected from the world's prime estates, and your teapot will be regularly replenished or replaced with a different choice of leaf. This is a relaxing venue to be recommended for a delicious, most satisfactory afternoon tea.

THE WOLSELEY

$\mathcal{E}$ver since the Wolseley opened its doors in November 2003, it has gained a reputation as one of the most stylish restaurants in London. It is hard to believe that this magnificent Grade II listed building was originally designed in the 1920s as a prestigious car showroom for the eponymous Wolseley Motors Ltd., with the grand pillars, high ceilings, marble floors where the cars were displayed, sweeping staircases, and loggias. By 1927 the building had changed hands and become home to a branch of Barclays Bank, who had specialised furniture designed for them, including a post box and stamp machine, which are still on display today. Now, however, the Wolseley is a Grand Café, and the place is glitzy and positively hums with activity all day long, so don't expect to sit in peace and quiet here.

ADDRESS: 160 Piccadilly,
St James's, London W1J 9EB

TEL: +44 (0)20 7499 6996

EMAIL:
reservations@thewolseley.com

WEB: www.thewolseley.com

AFTERNOON TEA SERVED:
Monday to Friday 3.00pm–6.30pm,
Saturday 3.30pm–5.30pm,
Sunday 3.30pm–6.30pm.
December times vary.

SET TEAS: cream tea, traditional
tea, champagne tea

**NEAREST UNDERGROUND
STATIONS:** Green Park

**PLACES OF INTEREST
NEARBY:** Green Park, The Royal
Academy, Burlington Arcade,
Fortnum & Mason

The staff are very attentive, and will happily bring you a newspaper whilst you wait for your dining companions to arrive. When you are ready to commence, afternoon tea is served in the tea room and the main restaurant. The set afternoon tea, on its tiered stand, is as traditional as it comes. There are a variety of finger sandwiches, excellent fruit scones, and an ever-changing selection of pastries and cakes. You can opt for just scones and clotted cream, or even just cake and tea, but that would rather miss the point of afternoon tea! The small selection of leaf teas includes the Wolseley's own afternoon blend, English breakfast, Earl Grey, Darjeeling, Ceylon, Assam, jasmine, and green. A favourite with celebrities, you never know who you might be sitting next to.

Credits

All images courtesy and copyright of the respective venues in the book, except as follows: pages 14, 15 (bottom), The Ampersand/©Amy Murrell; pages 18–21, ©Galvin at the Athenaeum; page 22, Balthazar/©David Loftus and pages 23–24, Balthazar/High Five Afternoon Tea ©John Carey; pages 88–91, ©Grosvenor House, A JW Marriott Hotel; pages 92–93, Ham Yard Hotel/©Simon Brown; pages 112–114, The Ivy, Chelsea Garden/©Paul Winch-Furness; pages 115–116, The Ivy Café, St John's Wood/©Paul Winch-Furness; pages 124, 126 (top), and 127, The Langham/©Paul Judd Food Photography; pages 145–146, Number Sixteen/©Simon Brown; page 178, The Savoy/©Victoria Metaxas; pages 190–191, The Soho Hotel/©Simon Brown; pages 195–196, St Pancras Renaissance Hotel/©London Marriott Hotel County Hall; pages 200 and 202, The Wallace Restaurant/©Chris Orange; pages 203–204, The Wellesley, Knightsbridge/©Susannah Fields; page 206, The Wolseley/©Nick Ingram.

Recipes courtesy and copyright of the named venue/creator and recipe images courtesy and copyright of the venue unless specified otherwise: pages 16–17, The Ampersand/Sezwin Mascarenhas; pages 70–71, Egerton House Hotel/Bea Tollman; pages 78–79, Four Seasons Hotel, Park Lane/David Oliver; pages 86–87, The Goring/Shay Cooper; pages 110–111, InterContinental London, Park Lane; pages 122–123, The Lanesborough; pages 128–129, The Langham, photo by Paul Judd Photography; pages 138–139, The Milestone Hotel/Bea Tollman; pages 150–151, Old Parsonage Hotel; pages 170–171, The Rubens at the Palace/Bea Tollman.

Miscellaneous images courtesy and copyright of the respective venues and photographers. cover, courtesy of The Orangery at Kensington Palace; back cover top left, The Connaught; back cover top right, Brigit's Bakery; back cover top middle left, Hotel du Vin, Henley-on-Thames; back cover bottom middle left, Balthazar/High Five Afternoon Tea ©John Carey; back cover bottom left, The Ned; page 3, Brigit's Bakery; page 4, The Soho Hotel/©Simon Brown; page 5 top left, Brigit's Bakery; page 5 bottom left, The Milestone Hotel; page 5 right, Conrad London St James; page 6 left, The Wallace Restaurant; page 6 right, The Berkeley; page 7 right, Number Sixteen/©Simon Brown; page 8 top left, The Rubens at the Palace; page 8 top right, Hotel du Vin, Henley-on-Thames; page 8 bottom left, Conrad London St James; page 8 bottom middle, Egerton House Hotel; page 8 bottom right, The Ivy Café, St John's Wood; page 9 left, The Stafford; page 9 right, The Connaught.

Index

11 Cadogan Gardens, 12–13

afternoon teas. *See also specific locales*
  high society and, 6
  magical, mystical tea and, 6–7
  map of London venues, 8–9
  origins and evolution of, 6–7
  overview of London options, 3–5
  popularity today, 7
  range of food and drink offerings, 3
  recipes for. *See* recipes
  timing of, 3
Amaranto Lounge, at Four Seasons Hotel, Park Lane, 76–77

Ampersand, 14–15

Belgravia, The Lanesborough, 119–21
Berkshire
  Cliveden House (Taplow), 45–47
  Coworth Park (Ascot), 59–61
  Hotel du Vin, Henley-on-Thames, 101–3
Bloomsbury, The Bloomsbury, 31–32
boat and bus tours, Brigit's Bakery Afternoon Tea and, 35–37
breads. *See* recipes
bus and boat tours, Brigit's Bakery Afternoon Tea and, 35–37

cakes. *See* recipes
Cambridgeshire, Hotel du Vin, Cambridge, 97–99
Céleste, at The Lanesborough, 119–21
Chelsea
  11 Cadogan Gardens, 12–13
  The Ivy, Chelsea Garden, 113–14
City of London, The Ned, 143–44
Clerkenwell, Four Seasons Hotel, Ten Trinity Square, 81–82
The Collins Room, at The Berkeley, 25–27
Covent Garden
  Balthazar, 23–24